The Year of the Poet VII

of the

January 2020

The Poetry Posse

inner child press, ltd.

The Poetry Posse 2020

Gail Weston Shazor
Shareef Abdur Rasheed
Teresa E. Gallion
hülya n. yılmaz
Kimberly Burnham
Tzemin Ition Tsai
Elizabeth Esguerra Castillo
Jackie Davis Allen
Joe Paire
Caroline 'Ceri' Nazareno
Ashok K. Bhargava
Alicja Maria Kuberska
Swapna Behera
Albert 'Infinite' Carrasco
Eliza Segiet
William S. Peters, Sr.

~ * ~

In order to maintain each poet's authentic voice, this volume has not undergone the scrutiny of editing. Please take time to indulge each contributor for their own creativity and aspirations to convey their uniqueness.

hülya n. yılmaz, Ph.D.
Director of Editing
Inner Child Press International

General Information

The Year of the Poet VII
January 2020 Edition

The Poetry Posse

1st Edition : 2020

Publisher Information
1st Edition : Inner Child Press
intouch@innerchildpress.com
www.innerchildpress.com

ISBN-13 : 978-1-970020-90-8 (inner child press, ltd.)

$ 12.99

WHAT WOULD LIFE BE WITHOUT A LITTLE POETRY?

$\mathcal{D}$edication

This Book is dedicated to

Humanity, Peace & Poetry

the Power of the Pen

can effectuate change!

&

The Poetry Posse

past, present & future

our Patrons and Readers

the Spirit of our Everlasting Muse

In the darkness of my life
I heard the music
I danced . . .
and the Light appeared
and I dance

Janet P. Caldwell

Table of Contents

Foreword   *ix*

Preface   *xi*

Jean Henry Dunant &Frédéric Passy   *xv*

The Poetry Posse

Gail Weston Shazor   1

Alicja Maria Kuberska   7

Jackie Davis Allen   15

Tezmin Ition Tsai   21

Shareef Abdur – Rasheed   27

Kimberly Burnham   35

Elizabeth Esguerra Castillo   41

Joe Paire   47

hülya n. yılmaz   53

Teresa E. Gallion   61

Table of Contents . . . *continued*

Ashok K. Bhargava   67

Caroline Nazareno   73

Swapna Behera   79

Albert Carassco   87

Eliza Segiet   93

William S. Peters, Sr.   99

January's Featured Poets   107

B S Tyagi   109

Andy Scott   115

Ashok Chakravarthy Tholana   123

Anwer Ghani   129

Inner Child News   137

Other Anthological Works   163

Foreword

A new decade dawns with poetry and wisdom. This is our collective poetry posse's seventh year publishing *The Year of The Poet* with a book a month from Inner Child Press. It has been our great privilege to share much beauty and soothe pain with words of insight and laughter, words that rhythm and dance across the page, bouncing off into the reader's heart.

Each year we contemplate a theme, delving into ideas, finding words to describe feelings, conflicts, relationships and growth. This year may our vision be 20-20 as we contemplate the words and ideas of Nobel Peace Prize winners. And may we share our understanding of the world and how-to live-in peace with each other in a way that goes deep and touches what is real, raw, powerful and magnificent.

There are as many ways to win a Nobel Peace Prize as there are ways to find peace in this world. In January, we celebrate the 1901 prize shared by two Europeans: Jean Henry Dunant (Swiss) and Frédéric Passy (French). Dunant found peace in compassion for the wounded of all nations on all sides of each war. He founded the Red Cross. Passy felt that peace is found in economic justice and free trade. He was dubbed the "dean" of the international peace movement.

A shout out to Martin Luther King, Jr. who would have been 91 this month and won the Nobel Peace Prize in 1964 for his non-violent opposition to discrimination.

This year of poetry is an opportunity to think about what we have learned from world history and our own personal experiences of peace, compassion, security and justice. It is an opportunity to contemplate how we respond to conflict, injustice and violence, how it changes us and how we grow in the aftermath of life's challenges.

May we all find peace in poetry and in the day to day of life in 2020 wherever in the world we find ourselves. Happy New Year.

Kimberly Burnham
Spokane, Washington

Preface

Dear Family and Friends,

Yes I am excited and feel accomplished as we enter our seventh year of publishing what I and many others deem to be a worthy enterprise, *The Year of the Poet*.

This past year we have aligned our vision with that of Nober Peace Prize Recipients. We have title this year's theme. The Year of Peace! Hopefully thorugh our sharing each month, our poetry can have a profound effect on our global consciousness and the need for peace while educating ourselves and our readership about some of the individuals who have made history through their efforts to promulgate peace for all of humanity.. We are on our way to hitting yet another milestone. Needless to say, I am elated.

To reiterate, our initial vision was to just perform at this level for the year of 2014. Since that time we have had the blessed opportunity to include many other wonderful poets, word artists and storytellers in the Poetry Posse from lands, cultures and persuasions all over the world. We have featured hundreds of additional poets, thereby introducing their poetic offerings to our vast global audience.

In keeping with our effort and vision to expand the awareness of poets from all walks by making this offerings accessible, we at Inner Child Press International will continue to make every volume a FREE Download. The books are also available for purchase at the affordable cost of $7.00 per volume.

In the previous years, our monthly themes were Flowers, Birds, Gemstones, Trees and Past Cultures. This coming year we have elected to continue our focus of choosing what we consider a significant subject . . . PEACE! In each month's volume you will have the opportunity to not only read at least one poem themed by our Poetry Posse members about such celebrated Peace Ambassadors, but we have included a few words about each individual in our prologue. We hope you find the poetic offerings insightful as we use our poetic form to relay to you what we too have learned through our research in making our offering available to you, our readership.

In closing, we would like to thank you for being an integral part of our amazing journey.

Enjoy our amazing featured poets . . . they are amazing!

Building Cultural Bridges of Understanding . . .

Bless Up . . . From the home in our hearts to yours

Bill

The Poetry Posse
Inner Child Press Ineternational

PS

Do Not forget about the World Healing, World
Peace Poetry effort.

Available here

www.worldhealingworldpeacepoetry.com

**For Free Downloads of Previous Issues of
The Year of the Poet**

www.innerchildpress.com/the-year-of-the-poet

World Healing, World Peace Foundation
human beings for humanity

worldhealingworldpeacefoundation.org

Jean Henry Dunant
&
Frédéric Passy

Each month for the year of 2020, which we have deemed as *The Year of Peace*, we at Inner Child Press International will be celebrating through our poetry a few Nobel Peace Prize Recipients who have contributed greatly to humanity via their particular avocations. This month you will find select poems from each Poetry Posse member on this month's celebrants. In 1901, the award was jointly given to French pacifist Frédéric Passy, founder of the Peace League and Dunant, founder of the Red Cross.

For more information about visit :

www.nobelpeaceprize.org/Prize-winners/Prizewinner-documentation/Jean-Henry-Dunant-Frederic-Passy

Poets . . .
sowing seeds in the
Conscious Garden of Life,
that those who have yet to come
may enjoy the Flowers.

Poets, Writers . . . know that we are the enchanting magicians that nourishes the seeds of dreams and thoughts . . . it is our words that entice the hearts and minds of others to believe there is something grand about the possibilities that life has to offer and our words tease it forth into action . . . for you are the Poet, the Writer to whom the Gift of Words has been entrusted . . .

~ wsp

poetry is . . .

Poetry succeeds where instruction fails.

~ wsp

I Fly

because

...said the Dreamer to the world.

I Can

www.iamjustbill.com

Gail Weston Shazor

This is a creative promise ~ my pen will speak to and for the world. Enamored with letters and respectful of their power, I have been writing for most of my life. A mother, daughter, sister and grandmother I give what I have been given, greatfilledly.

Author of . . .

"An Overstanding of an Imperfect Love"
&
Notes from the Blue Roof

Lies My Grandfathers Told Me

available at Inner Child Press.

www.facebook.com/gailwestonshazor
www.innerchildpress.com/gail-weston-shazor
navypoet1@gmail.com

A Red Cross

Peace

Bears not

The passing

Of pigment borne

Under any flag

And yet we all shall live

In disgraceful prejudice

When called to serve one another

On battlefields real and imagined

In which our lives cannot help but cross

Double Ought Chambers

Is peace solved in halls or wars

Indoors or out

In hearts or on skin

There is no solution for peace

We cannot simply

Talk ourselves into peace

Or subdue ourselves into peace

We cannot make others into peace

We have to be peace

Diamante

Peace

Relieved, splendid

Wanting, loving, needing

We have always tried

Failing, solving, making,

Thoughtless, obnoxious

Failures

Alicja Maria Kuberska

Alicja Maria Kuberska

Alicja Maria Kuberska – awarded Polish poetess, novelist, journalist, editor. She was born in 1960, in Świebodzin, Poland. She now lives in Inowrocław, Poland.

In 2011 she published her first volume of poems entitled: "The Glass Reality". Her second volume "Analysis of Feelings", was published in 2012. The third collection "Moments" was published in English in 2014, both in Poland and in the USA. In 2014, she also published the novel - "Virtual roses" and volume of poems "On the border of dream". Next year her volume entitled "Girl in the Mirror" was published in the UK and "Love me" , " (Not)my poem" in the USA. In 2015 she also edited anthology entitled "The Other Side of the Screen".

In 2016 she edited two volumes: "Taste of Love" (USA), "Thief of Dreams" (Poland) and international anthology entitled " Love is like Air" (USA). In 2017 she published volume entitled "View from the window" (Poland). She also edits series of anthologies entitled "Metaphor of Contemporary" (Poland)

Her poems have been published in numerous anthologies and magazines in Poland, the USA, the UK, Albania, Belgium, Chile, Spain, Israel, Canada, India, Italy, Uzbekistan, Czech Republic, South Korea and Australia. She was a featured poet of New Mirage Journal (USA) in the summer of 2011.

Alicja Kuberska is a member of the Polish Writers Associations in Warsaw, Poland and IWA Bogdani, Albania. She is also a member of directors' board of Soflay Literature Foundation.

We are all brothers

Suffering and death have no nationality.
Empathy does not allow indifference.
Jean Henry Dunant saw suffering brothers
in the wounded soldiers of the enemy army.

The enormity of misfortune crushed hostility.
The church in nearby Castiglione
took in the dying and mutilated.
The words 'tutti fratelli' were said there
and blood soaking on the bandage
made the sign of the cross

The book "Remembrance of Solferino"
like the sound of a great bell
woke up the dormant consciences.
Belief in humanity returned
and it called to the battlefields
hosts of white angels.
They brought hope for survival

The man rich in spirit started
to live in the shelter for the poor.
Many beautiful ideas
were struck down
and poverty together with oblivion
wrote a grim script

The journalist's voice moved hearts.
Ashamed Europe admitted
the first Nobel Peace Prize.

Little girl

Until yesterday she believed in fairy tales.
Elves were hidden among the rose bushes
And she looked for a good fairy
Ensconced in the thicket of the flowering trees.

In that world
She painted a rainbow on soap bubbles
And she thought that good always wins over evil.

Don't cry stupid.
He is a rich man and you won't have a bad time
- mother hissed in her ear like the snake in paradise .

She was afraid of this old man with a sticky look,
Who spun threads like a huge spider
To trap her in a cocoon of his big fingers.

At night, a desperate scream shattered the silence.
The white dress transformed into blood-red.
An orphaned teddy- bear cried in her family home.

My India

I loved India unconditionally
with all its pros and cons
like mother her baby

I miss and I come back in my dreams
to the land of maharajas,
which is decked like a peacock in rich sari
and buzzing bracelets.
I long also for the poor houses of Old Delhi
where the poverty sleeps on the doorsteps.

I will remember
the rickshaw speaking with a British accent,
Jaipur sparkling with gems,
silks shining on stalls,
Taj Mahal similar to a tear
enchanted in white marble
and to despair carved in stone.

A thin trail of smoke
rising from incense
and writhing like a cobra,
a little garam masala in rice
taste of cardamom in my cup of tea
shawl thrown over my shoulders
is all I need
to bring my memories back to life

Only there a man can see
man's symbiosis with nature,
harmony emerging from chaos,
interpenetration of death and life

in the eternal cycle of reincarnation,
the cradle of languages and ancient culture
immortalized in Sanskrit and the Vedas.

My India will stay in me.
I absorbed it with all my senses,
it blended into my heart and mind.
  It is like an insect inside the Baltic amber
and like a ticket to my dreams.

Alicja Maria Kuberska

Jackie
Davis
Allen

Jackie Davis Allen

Jackie Davis Allen, otherwise known as Jacqueline D. Allen or Jackie Allen, grew up in the Cumberland Mountains of Appalachia. As the next eldest daughter of a coal miner father and a stay at home mother, she was the first in her family to attend and graduate from college. Her siblings, in their own right, are accomplished, though she is the only one, to date, that has discovered the gift of writing.

Graduating from Radford University, with a Bachelors of Science degree in Early Education, she taught in both public and private schools. For over a decade she taught private art classes to children both in her home and at a local Art and Framing Shop where she also sold her original soft sculptured Victorian dolls and original christening gowns.

She resides in northern Virginia with her husband, taking much needed get-aways to their mountain home near the Blue Ridge Mountains, a place that evokes memories of days spent growing up in the Appalachian Mountains.

A lover of hats, she has worn many. Following marriage to her college sweetheart, and as wife, mother, grandmother, teacher, tutor, artist, writer, poet and crafter, she is a lover of art and antiques, surrounding herself, always, with books, seeking to learn more.

In 2015 she authored *Looking for Rainbows, Poetry, Prose and Art*, and in 2017, *Dark Side of the Moon*. Both books of mostly narrative poetry were published by Inner Child Press and were edited by hulya n. yilmaz.

in 2019, No Illusions.Through the Looking Glass, which was nominated to be considered for a Pulitzer Prize by the publisher and editor of InnerChild Press, ltd.

http://www.innerchildpress.com/jackie-davis-allen.php
jackiedavisallen.com

1901 The First Nobel Prize Winners: Jean Henry Dunant and Frederic Passy

Dunant recorded his impressions, wove together
the threads of his experiences, searching for a way,
the means to care for wounded soldiers.

A Memory of Solferino, his book, the result,
became the inspiration for creation, in 1863
for the International Committee of the Red Cross.

Initiated or not, it, in 1864 his book became
the inspiration for the Geneva Convention, an organization
to care for wounded soldiers of the Civil War.

Certainly, Jean Henry Dunant, a Swiss man,
was not aware nor even thinking, that in 1901
he'd be awarded the first ever Nobel Peace Prize.

And neither would Frederick Passy, a Frenchman.
He was to share the first ever Nobel Peace Prize with
Henry Dunant, for his work in the peace movement.

Passy, like Dunant, was a fervent activist for peace;
Passy being recognized as both author and politician.
And as the "dean of European peace activists".

Selfless, working for peace, neither man sought fame nor
acclaim for their efforts, and yet, highly deserving, they
received the first ever Nobel Peace Prize. We thank you.

Starting Over

Cold and brown
lies the earth beneath a coat of snow
and yet the scene emerges
as a thing of beauty.

On stark and peeling branches
a red cardinal sweetly sings its song.

Mistakes and should-have's
haunt and rattle my repose;
long is the list of regrettable acts
that blight and stain my soul.

Unmasked, I offer a sincere apology
to each and everyone I've wronged.

A chance at renewal
greets me like a blast of cold wind;
I pray for forgiveness
and am awakened, ready to begin again.

From this day forward, with God's help,
may I begin to sing new and better songs.

a million stars in the sky

the salty breeze kissed the night with the gentle art
of passion's melody and with hearts rising and sighing

it was as if one was looking back
on love's reflective shore
the dawn coming ever nearer
to the sandy beach

the saltwater tides were rising
and falling, the crashing waves, too,
in syncopation
with the lovers

their songs mimicked
the wind's wild cry
while caressing midst
the sea-foam's froth kissed mist
in passion's blissful estate, they bathed
thinking of little else
other than intimacy's gift
as love guided their innocent wistful wishes

they thought then
they think now, that they were witnessing a million stars
waking up the sky

Tzemin Ition Tsai

Dr. Tzemin Ition Tsai (蔡澤民博士) was born in Republic of China, in 1957. He holds a Ph.D. in Chemical Engineering and two Masters of Science in Applied Mathematics and Chemical Engineering. He is a professor at Asia University (Taiwan), editor of "Reading, Writing and Teaching" academic text. He also writes the long-term columns for Chinese Language Monthly in Taiwan.

He is a scholar with a wide range of expertise, while maintaining a common and positive interest in science, engineering and literature member. He is also an editor of "Reading, Writing and Teaching" academic text and a columnist for *'Chinese Language Monthly'* in Taiwan

He has won many national literary awards. His literary works have been anthologized and published in books, journals, and newspapers in more than 40 countries and have been translated into more than a dozen languages.

"The Should Not" As The Centuries Moving Silently

Like other "isms"
Lofty goals
Hide deep contradictions
There is not one humanitarianism, but several
Dominated Face
Save and protect lives when disaster strikes
The blindness is a telling indicator of its strong
isomorphism
'you' can join 'us' on our terms
But don't expect any consideration.
If you don't

In addition to being
An ideology, a movement, a profession
And
A compassionate endeavor
In which actors compete for market share
Humanitarian action also expanded accordion-style into
new territories
The northern/western tip of the iceberg
The first line of defense for the most vulnerable
A banner that is used to justify a multitude of interventions
Two "souls" in the humanitarian

One focusing on the universal values of compassion and
charity
One focusing on change and transformation of society
A form of containment in the last 20 years
Is nothing new
Have crossed the threshold of power and shall return to this
later
Predictions are always dangerous
Especially about the future

When humanitarian action has drifted away from its
principled moorings
We would need much bigger ears, smaller mouths
It seems the end of a myth

Tzemin Ition Tsai

Shareef
Abdur
Rasheed

Shareef Abdur Rasheed

Shareef Abdur-Rasheed, AKA Zakir Flo was born and raised in Brooklyn, New York. His education includes Brooklyn College, Suffolk County Community College and Makkah, Saudi Arabia. He is a Veteran of the Viet Nam era, where in 1969 he reverted to his now reverently embraced Islamic Faith. He is very active in the Islamic community and beyond with his teachings, activism and his humanity.

Shareef's spiritual expression comes through the persona of "Zakir Flo". Zakir is Arabic for "To remind". Never silent, Shareef Abdur-Rasheed is always dropping science, love, consciousness and signs of the time in rhyme.

Shareef is the Patriarch of the Abdur-Rasheed Family with 9 Children (6 Sons and 3 Daughters) and 41 Grandchildren (24 Boys and 17 Girls).

For more information about Shareef, visit his personal FaceBook Page at :

https://www.facebook.com/shareef.abdurrasheed1
https://zakirflo.wordpress.com

Peace..,
----

was their objective
dedicated their lives
in pursuit of
Federic Passy,
Henry Dunant
both Europeans
Passy French
Dunant Swiss
Passy, economist,
pacifist
Dunant, humanitarian,
social activist
Passy founded many
peace organizations
in Europe
worked tirelessly to
establish peace in Europe
believed dialog, education
in social sciences to dispel
ignorance, fear that stoked
flames of war in Europe
and beyond
this was a precursor
that later lead to
League of Nations,
then United Nations
Dunant developed medical
provisions for the wounded
in battle
helped organize the first
Geneva convention
to enhance aid and rights
of wounded warriors
these efforts laid the

groundwork to him co-
founding the Red Cross
both shared the first
nobel peace prize in 1901

food4thought = education

so they..,

----

don't stop running jibs
but substance not there
to give
it's more of the same lame
BS with different names,
topics usually vary
not lately though
but the theme remains
the same
maintain status quo
that be the stations cash flo
and the same for those who
pose for the cameras and
the public image dem project
but substance dem forget
not in their agenda ever
not a speck to be found
that in any respect
remotely resembles
profound real progress
in quality of life vis-a-vis
community, solidarity,
humans in harmony
real healthy society
just more of the samo,
same bull$#!+ variety
meanwhile folks seem
to grin and bear with a smile
as the nation gets in position
to join history's pile
of former empires

who had their day in the sun
but now their gone, forgotten,
done
they all waved their flags
but now dem nothing but rags
to wipe that a$$
glory belongs only to the one who
created you
caution all nations
praise the creator not the creation
put your flags down
raise up your hands

food4thought = education

dribble..,

----

drips from cracked lips
dem trip over obvious fibs
constantly flip the script
in fact dem not fibs
why?
dem lies, straight up lies
every time dem move
lips
what comes out?
nothing but straight up lies
so dem tomb say " here
lay the liar "
destined to the fire
detested honesty, ridiculed
morality
mistook criminality for bravery
thought truthfulness crazy
in his grave dreads the day
called judgement
when all the lies will be
brought in front of us
exposed
impose penalty
under authority of all mighty
no where to fly away and hide
on that day
only truth will abide

food4thought = education

Kimberly Burnham

Kimberly Burnham

A brain health expert with a PhD in Integrative Medicine, Kimberly Burnham has lived in tropical Colombia; in Belgium during the Vietnam War; in Japan teaching businessmen English; in diverse international Toronto, Canada and several places in the US. Now, she's in Spokane, WA with her wife, Elizabeth, two sets of twins (age 11 & 14) and three dogs. Her recent book, *Awakenings: Peace Dictionary, Language and the Mind, a Daily Brain Health Program* includes the word for peace in hundreds of languages. Kim's poetry weaves through 70 volumes of *The Year of the Poet, Inspired by Gandhi, Women Building the World, A Woman's Place in the Dictionary*, Tiferet Journal, Human/Kind Journal and more.

https://www.nervewhisperer.solutions/
https://www.linkedin.com/in/kimberlyburnham/

Jean Henry Dunant

A small book
a memory of solferino
an unknown man his ideas destine for greatness
describes the battle itself
the battlefield after the bloody fight
the chaotic disorder
sharing unspeakable despair
and the story of the efforts
to care for the wounded
result in a plan

Nations of the world
provide care for wartime wounded
train volunteers to nurse
all equally this side and that
Henry Dunant founding the Red Cross
nudging twelve nations to sign the Geneva Convention
under a red cross on a field of white
for which the Swiss Dunant shared
in the 1901 Nobel Peace Prize

Aftermath

Some achieve greatness in the aftermath
when the war
divorce
election is done
decided
settled

Like Jean Henry Dunant
founding the Red Cross
in the aftermath of the battle of Solferino
winning the 1901 Nobel Peace Prize
remembered
long after the battle forgotten
forged in blood and chaos
emerging under a red cross
on a protective white field

Surrounded by peace in the languages
of his native Switzerland frieden
friede fréda fridde
fridn sholem paix
paz pas patz
pace paas péx
pasch and kotor

Peace and Free Trade

Frédéric Passy dubbed the "dean"
of the international peace movement
saw free trade as a pathway to peace
over 200 years ago
before the conflict between
a united Sweden and Norway peaked
before World War I and World War II
before the current trade wars
bringing the question
what have we learned?
in 200 years about fairness compassion
and creating peace out of goods

Elizabeth E. Castillo

Elizabeth Esguerra Castillo

Elizabeth Esguerra Castillo is a multi-awarded and an Internationally-Published Contemporary Author/Poet and a Professional Writer / Creative Writer / Feature Writer / Journalist / Travel Writer from the Philippines. She has 2 published books, "Seasons of Emotions" (UK) and "Inner Reflections of the Muse", (USA). Elizabeth is also a co-author to more than 60 international anthologies in the USA, Canada, UK, Romania, India. She is a Contributing Editor of Inner Child Magazine, USA and an Advisory Board Member of Reflection Magazine, an international literary magazine. She is a member of the American Authors Association (AAA) and PEN International.

Web links:

Facebook Fan Page

https://free.facebook.com/ElizabethEsguerraCastillo

Google Plus

https://plus.google.com/u/0/+ElizabethCastillo

A Memory of Solferino

Jean Henry Dunant, a witness of a raging battle,
Soldiers taking the lives of their own
Maiming and wounding each other,
With all these sufferings he must make a stand
And out of his golden heart aided the sick and wounded.

A Memory of Solferino-
Depicting a labyrinth of lost souls
The wounded with their woes and pleas,
Echoing the vastness of the hospital hallways
Where the deepest known sadness dwells.

Dunant, the Founder of the Red Cross,
Advocated for the protection and humane treatment of the
    ill
His life being committed to the aid of ailing people,
Was duly recognized, a much-deserved Noble Peace Prize.

Indigo Child

i am not of this world -
i came from an abysmal chaos-
but from this beautiful chaos, Desiderata was born-
a child of the Universe, precious and golden
a lovely old soul beyond time and space-
often misunderstood by mediocre minds-
but applauded by great free thinkers -
i long for a world enveloped in serenity-
inhabited by empaths with great sensitivity
a loner I may be but this is who I am-
but i've got this deep connection with things around me
an indigo girl at birth-
my temporary sanctuary is the Earth
lone wolves gather at my feet-
for i am their Goddess in human form.

Peace is Possible

We dream of a world enveloped in peace
Where people from all walks of life live
In dire harmony, love, and understanding,
A world where war does not even exist
A place of serenity, noble lives shared.

Peace is possible if we only take action
Let go of selfish ego and have the will to be selfless
Be like a child once more, full of hope and promises
And spread only love for all mankind
Wherever we may roam on earth.

The dove of peace with its immaculate white feathers
Can be seen hovering over the beauteous skies above
The promise of tomorrow, full of wonders and triumph
As we defeat all hindrances to attaining authentic peace
Peace which is longed for by hearts so pure
Awaiting of the dawning of a new frontier.

Joe
Paire

Joe Paire

Joseph L Paire' aka Joe DaVerbal Minddancer . . .
is a quiet man, born in a time where civil liberties
were a walk on thin ice. He's been a victim of his
own shyness often sidelined in his own quest for
love. He became the observer, charting life's path.
Taking note of the why, people do what they do. His
writings oft times strike a cord with the
dormant strings of the reader. His pen the rosined
bow drawn across the mind. He comes full-frontal
or in the subtlest way, always expressing in a way
that stimulate the senses.

www.facebook.com/joe.minddancer

Peace Rise

There is nothing so noble as to want peace for a nation
You don't even have to live there just care about creation
Two men on the street fighting do we stop and watch
or do we stop and stop the warring nations
Jean Henry Dunant thought so and laid it out in a
summation,
we now have the Red Cross and the Geneva convention
intervention of the peaceful kind in unpeaceful times
The first of two men to share the noble peace prize

There is nothing so noble as to want peace for a nation
You don't even have to live there just care about creation
Have you ever gone next door to borrow a cup of sugar
Would you if tariffs were in the way
Frederic Passy had a little something to say
The Inter-Parliamentary Union, the French Peace Society
There were still politicians who cared back in the day
Peace achieved by two men through different channels
Neither of them were sought honor to place on mantels
It was the right thing to do, it was the nice thing to do
in 1901 the Noble Peace Prize honored two.

A Good Day For Trade

Farmers and manufacturers stand up and cheer
Foreign trade is a known road to peace
Peace is the place we struggle to be at
A feast at the table with a whole lot left
I have two but only need one
Do I hoard it or export it let me ponder this some
My friend across the pond has the same situation
He has two but only needs one time for negotiations
Safe passage for our packages no tariffs to rattle this
Oh it's a great day for trade, and free trade equals peace
A Noble Peace Prize was awarded for such just a deed
We can achieve peace through many means
By any means may be necessary but contrary to war
I believe in what I'm here for, Peace Through Poetry
I know it's we the people, I'm just one seedling
Planted in this ground to be a sequel of ever-growing
PEACE.

Simply Out Of Love

It's snowing on an open road no lights and a tire blows
No flares no spare, who's out there
a total stranger pulls up in a bucket of rust
He found a tire amongst his rubble
So many people drove by just living in their bubbles
He stopped out of love for a fellow man in trouble
Voice of the voiceless is the poet
choice of the soul you have to look above man
We love man, we teach we feed, we preach we seed
We live and breathe to help each other
Everyone's a child everyone's a mother
Even those who live alone find love in their cover
I wrote a love poem out of misery
I wrote a mystery out of love
There's a constant common denominator
I'm always thinking of
what is it that I do simply out of love?

hülya
n.
yılmaz

hülya n. yılmaz

Liberal Arts Emerita, hülya n. yılmaz is a published author, literary translator, and Co-Chair and Director of Editing Services at Inner Child Press International. Her poetic work appeared in an excess of eighty-five anthologies of global endeavors and has been presented at numerous national and international poetry events. In 2018, the Writer's International Network of British Colombia, Canada honored yılmaz with a literary award. As of 2017, two of her poems remain permanently installed in *Telepoem Booth* – a U.S.-wide poetic art exhibition. hülya finds it vital for everyone to understand a deeper sense of self, and writes creatively to attain a comprehensive awareness for and development of our humanity.

Writing Web Site
https://hulyanyilmaz.com/

Editing Web Site
https://hulyasfreelancing.com

Money and a Famed Name

He is said to have lived a life of contrasts
from the year of 1828 to that of 1910.
A wealthy family,
A thriving business,
A Nobel Peace Prize . . .

None mattered
even before death came.
For John Henry Dunant, that is.

We all die alone.
Whether surrounded by family or friends,
to our final journey, we do go solo.

His was a faith of dying alone,
being carried to the grave "like a dog".
Though per his wish . . .

Contradictions to common convictions?

Not one penny spent
from all that which to others
was what his 1901-recognition meant . . .
His passionate commitment to humanitarianism
left behind a meaningful gift,
a "free bed".
Only the hospital
where his treatment took place
was to benefit . . .

Contradictions to common convictions?

What, in his reality,
was John Henry Dunant about?
We will never know.
Whoever conceived his life
to look like on ink,
had the last word, after all.

Honored

A phone call?
A knock on the door?
A fancy letter in the mail?

What difference does it make
when the world's most prestigious peace prize
appears at your doorstep one day?

Why would it ever matter
if it does not?

peace-HAIKU

not only for self

humanity needs it most

i feel, at what cost?

hülya n. yılmaz

Teresa E. Gallion

Teresa E. Gallion

Teresa E. Gallion was born in Shreveport, Louisiana and moved to Illinois at the age of 15. She completed her undergraduate training at the University of Illinois Chicago and received her master's degree in Psychology from Bowling Green State University in Ohio. She retired from New Mexico state government in 2012.

She moved to New Mexico in 1987. While writing sporadically for many years, in 1998 she started reading her work in the local Albuquerque poetry community. She has been a featured reader at local coffee houses, bookstores, art galleries, museums, libraries, Outpost Performance Space, the Route 66 Festival in 2001 and the State of Oklahoma's Poetry Festival in Cheyenne, Oklahoma in 2004. She occasionally hosts an open mic.

Teresa's work is published in numerous Journals and anthologies. She has two CDs: *On the Wings of the Wind* and *Poems from Chasing Light*. She has published three books: *Walking Sacred Ground, Contemplation in the High Desert* and *Chasing Light.*

Chasing Light was a finalist in the 2013 New Mexico/Arizona Book Awards.

The surreal high desert landscape and her personal spiritual journey influence the writing of this Albuquerque poet. When she is not writing, she is committed to hiking the enchanted landscapes of New Mexico. You may preview her work at

http://bit.ly/1aIVPNq or *http://bit.ly/13IMLGh*

Apostle of Peace

Frederic Passy one of the first
to receive the Nobel Peace Prize
earned the nickname, Apostle of Peace.

He was dedicated to the premise
that free trade between
independent nations promoted peace.

He founded the first French Peace Society.
An avid believer that peace through arbitration
and international co-operation is possible.

Passy was an activist for peace
throughout his life. After his death,
his agenda for peace was remembered.

First Day

Birth of the new day touches gently
and the wind gives a soft kiss.
Daybreak's brightness sparkles
in sleepy eyes.

Riding the morning chill is a
sacred experience. Shivers of
love roll up the spine.

This day is open to carve memories.
It is a blessing to participate
in new beginnings.

There is no better way to embrace
the landscape of a new year
then to kneel to the universe
as the first morning slides into my soul.

Teresa E. Gallion

Drizzle

Nature gives the sand a wet kiss.
A fine mist sprays the desert
with the moisture of love's rain
feeding the prolonged drought.

Arroyos flood the terrain,
leave mud pies of entertaining
shapes to tease the senses.
Rocks change positions.

Soft spots sink in the sand
as sunlight exposes itself.
An explosion of light
massages waves in the landscape.

Happy boots trek in solitude
heavy with fresh mud.
Light minds reflect on the splendor
that captures the day.

Ashok K. Bhargava

Ashok K. Bhargava

Ashok Bhargava is a poet, writer, community activist, public speaker, management consultant and a keen photographer. Based in Vancouver, he has published several collections of his poems: Riding the Tide, Mirror of Dreams, A Kernel of Truth, Skipping Stones, Half Open Door and Lost in the Morning Calm. His poetry has been published in various literary magazines and anthologies.

Ashok is a Poet Laureate and poet ambassador to Japan, Korea and India. He is founder of WIN: Writers International Network Canada. Its main objective is to inspire, encourage, promote and recognize writers of diverse genres, artists and community leaders. He has received many accolades including Nehru Humanitarian Award for his leadership of Writers International Network Canada, Poets without Borders Peace Award for his journeys across the globe to celebrate peace and to create alliances with poets, and Kalidasa Award for creative writings.

A New Dawn

It's first the intentional conflict
then war and thereafter
the fear of losing
and dying.

In the battlefield
there are only wounded
who blend, blur and bleed
into unknown blood drops
dripping through their eyes
turning mortality into a shadow and
the shadow into something else.

Every few minutes
at the threshold of death
some survivors gasp for air
then drift back down to the oblivion
without fully waking.

Their eyes
sense but can't see
a friend from a foe
until they breathe
the last breath.

*This poem is inspired by Jean Henry Dunant's book "A
Memory of Solferino" (1862) which lead to the creation of
a neutral organization to care for the wounded soldiers
called International Committee of the Red Cross (ICRC) in
1863.

Where has Humanity Gone

we are
the spirits of the long lost
humanity

> a promise of a new dawn
> surrounded by the darkness
> of the lethal wars

> peace
> in its entirety
> is anticipation of light
> and yet

there is no hope
for the agony
> we endure
> in every malicious moment

> because
> everything presumed empty
> is really overflowing
> with fullness

> and every
> fullness is empty
> in its core

* This poem is inspired by a show staged in 2010 by a
Japanese all-female musical theater troupe based in
Takarazuka city, on Jean Dunant's time in Solferino and
the founding of the Red Cross, titled Where has Humanity
Gone?

Resilience

The crowds flock to the shrines

like bees to the flowers

for the nectar.

And they remain oblivious

to the joys and despairs of

other dreamers.

I look for something

but what I seek

no longer exist here.

Caroline
'Ceri Naz'
Nazareno

Carolin 'Ceri' Nazareno

Caroline 'Ceri Naz' Nazareno-Gabis, World Poetry Canada International Director to Philippines is known as a 'poet of peace and friendship', a multi-awarded poet, editor, journalist, speaker, linguist, educator, peace and women's advocate. She believes that learning other's language and culture is a doorway to wisdom.

Among her poetic belts include 7 th Prize Winner in the 19 th and 20 th Italian Award of Literary Festival; Writers International Network-Canada "Amazing Poet 2015", The Frang Bardhi Literary Prize 2014 (Albania), the sair-gazeteci or Poet Journalist Award 2014 (Tuzla, Istanbul, Turkey) and World Poetry Empowered Poet 2013 (Vancouver, Canada). She's a featured member of Association of Women's Rights and Development (AWID), The Poetry Posse, Galaktika Poetike, Asia Pacific Writers and Translators (APWT), Axlepino and Anacbanua.

Her poetry and children's stories have been featured in different anthologies and magazines worldwide.

Links to her works:

panitikan.ph/2018/03/30/caroline-nazareno-gabis
apwriters.org/author/ceri_naz
www.aveviajera.org/nacionesunidasdelasletras/id1181
.html

Homage to the Nobel Peace Laureates
(Jean Henry Dunant and Frederick Passy)

You belong to the Legion of Honor
Noble twin towers of peace
In every nation you stood for,

Dunant, the humanist,
Etched a glorious soul
Amidst economic struggles
You've embroidered a trademark of flame
You are the voice of the wounded
As you are the true Epic of the Red Crescent!

Passy, the pacifist
The 'Apostle of Peace'
The chamber of your heart
Beats with a regal passion,
O' dean of the radiant peace
Nations accord, in the ideals
Of a monumental freedom.

Your names' emblem
A fulfilled a million dreams and visions.

The Dreamer's Note

Feel and seal the flow of your heart
Beaming lights in the horizon's pounding sound
Silence breaks in one's sleepless nights
Will there be new tomorrow's summer sand?

Midnight struck the Hades's gates
Zeus promulgates his creed againsts the fools
Hours of reading palms and false intentions
Lost in the dark, took its flight for the Zions.

There's glory for the life gained in pain
Serenity and truth in you of yous
Reality speaks when someone's love prevails
For the faith that heals, for blind's new brailles.

Anchor thy dreams to living seed of deeds
Pouring kindness in sharing gifts of weeds
True fate is in our own hands praying wand
Live to the fullest of best dreamer's stand.

Stygian Mills

I search for you
In the shadows, between the windows;
When the moonlit strikes right to my room
The mystical architecture that I long for,
Ablaze with the revolt of palm trees
Rustling through the beachfront,
Cinematically, I see the difference,
Your sheer dominance in my mind,
And I know it'll be my lifelong paramour.

Oh, that dream is beauty.

I search for you
In the distances, between the calendars
For I know when you're not here with me;
It'll be light years to finger-count,
A must see different story
I have written for today's musing,
It's all about you in galactic scale;
But my heart resists, to weigh you
'Cause you're all that matters,

To me, evermore.

I search for you 'til the dust runs out,
'til no morsels of pain I could feel,
'til all the wildcards to stay here with all your memories,
will leave me breathless.
'til our shadows conspire again,
In the new Space that we'll conceive once more.

Destiny gave me you, and me to you.

Swapna Behera

Swapna Behera is a bilingual contemporary poet, author, translator and editor from Odisha, India. She was a teacher from 1984 to 2015. Her stories, poems and articles are widely published in National and International journals, and ezines, and are translated into different national and International languages. She has penned six books. She is the recipient of the Prestigious International Mother Language UGADI AWARD WINNER 2019. She was conferred upon the Prestigious International Poesis Award of Honor at the 2nd Bharat Award for Literature as Jury in 2015, The Enchanting Muse Award in India World Poetree Festival 2017, World Icon of Peace Award in 2017, and the Pentasi B World Fellow Poet in 2017. She is the recipient of Gold Cross of Wisdom Award, the Prolific Poetess Award, The Life time Achievement Award, The Best Planner Award, The Sahitya Shiromani Award, ATAL BIHARI BAJPAYEE AWARD 2018, Ambassador De Literature Award 2018, Global Literature Guardian Award, International Life Time Achievement Award and the Master of Creative Impulse Award. She has received the Honoured Poet of India from the Seychelles Government accredited Literary Society LLSF. Her one poem A NIGHT IN THE REFUGEE CAMP is translated into 50 languages. She is the Ambassador of Humanity by Hafrikan Prince Art World Africa 2018 and an official member of World Nation's Writers Union, Kazakhstan 2018. Italy, the National President for India by Hispanomundial Union of Writers (UHE), Peru, the administrator of several poetic groups, and the Cultural Ambassador for India and south Asia of Inner Child Press U.S.

The Mystic Mariner

The mystic mariner
With the   vivacious smile
In the musical journey
Of his own cogent orbit

The mystic mariner
A spiral odyssey
Of the Ragas and Rasas
In the cat walk of the cosmic ramp

The mystic mariner
The catalogues of virgin eyes
Yet demonstrating peace
Peace decoding love
Love drifting oceans of empathy

Are you the musical seven notes,
reflected in the nature?
Or the interludes of
the baptised plasma?

The mystic mariner
His destination is a journey
With his astute aura
Entwining rainbow, polar stars
Butterflies in the horizon

The mystic mariner
reflects the incarnation within
His arena and aroma inscribes
In the pristine elixir

The mystic mariner
I bow for not that Thou Art
 in the mystic frame
But in a prolific protocol-----

At last they reached

at last they reached
to a circle of their own
when they listened to their leader
they stamped on the dot
of a ballot

at last they poured oil to their lamps
woke up whole night to receive wisdom ..

at last they reached the goal
their girls went to the school

 bicycles ran on the roads
illuminated versions started a road March

at last the cosy cuisine of love was served on every plate

the city remembered the prayers of indigenous ancients .

skills were preserved .

the listeners sat on every family
granny, the love guru of the family told stories
at last they spoke less , listened more .....
and
 reached the destination ..
where water was saved
Nature smiled ....
A pulsating secured zone celebrated peace........

Jean Henry Dunant and Red Cross

aftermath of each battle is so harrowing

it kills and gives penetration for generation
the torn visible pieces of flesh and invisible trauma
farmland becomes no man's land
the migration creates refugees
shocks for life time blurs a child's creativity ..

Henry Dunant the visionary and promoter
a great humanitarian
sees the pain   in body and soul
made the Red Cross movement
to put bandage on the wounds

the Italians ,French and Austrians killed each other
that was the aching memory of Solferino

Henry Dunant made the volunteers ready
the Red Cross team helped sick
 and wounded in the battle field
the medical teams always protected
in an agreement
all countries should help sick and wounded
that was the motto of Red cross
The emblem extends arms of equal length to all in the
battle field .
Henry Dunant got the noble peace .....

Swapna Behera

Albert 'Infinite' Carrasco

Albert "Infinite The Poet" Carrasco is an urban poet, mentor and public speaker.

Albert believes his experience of growing up in poverty, dealing with drugs and witnessing murder over and over were lessons learnt, in order to gain knowledge to teach. Albert's harsh reality and honesty is a powerfully packed punch delivered through rhyme. Infinite grew up in the east part of the Bronx and still resides there, so he knows many young men will follow the same dark path he followed looking for change. The life of crime should never be an option to being poor but it is, very often.

Infinite poetry @lulu.com

Alcarrasco2 on YouTube

Infinite the poet on reverbnation

Infinite Poetry

http://www.lulu.com/us/en/shop/al-infinite-carrasco/infinite-poetry/paperback/product-21040240.html

Jean Henry Dunant

Bullets fired wizzed by with intent of killing and maiming.
Bayonets thrust through bodies when there was no time for
aiming.
In the town of Solferino, Italian, Austrian and the French,
are inhaling the smell of ignited gunpowder as well as
rotting corpse stench.
Everyone is fighting for what they feel is right,
That's why your heard shots, screams and moans day and
night.
Mr. Dunant witnessed it all.
He had a good heart, He came up with the idea of getting
aid for all sick and wounded soldiers on the battle field
before they dearly depart.
He wrote a book and came up with a plan that every
country should have an association to reach out and give
those in need a hand.
Thousands upon thousands of lives that were saved during
wars would've been lost,
if it wasn't for Mr. Durant establishing the Red Cross.

Frédéric Passy

A scientist, politician and activist
He wasn't just worthy, he was a great laureate.
Passy founded the first French peace society,
And was also one of the founders of the inter parliamentary
union,
An organization for cooperation between elected
representatives of different countries.
Mr. Passy was an economist.
He wrote and that gave lectures on economic matters.
Passy put public opinion into action.
He believed in arbitration.
Instead of wars he believed there was other ways to settle
dispute between nations.
He wanted peace to be made,
And believed that countries would bond during free trade.
A half of century in the peace movement gave him the title,
"The Peace Apostle"

A product of my environment

it's a cold world so I kept the heater, dudes was getting hit left and right so I had to train myself to be an ambidextrous blazer. I'm walking the concrete Serengeti with two gats like Yosemite, if shit popped off I'm sending thirty four quickly, that's both sixteens with the two in the heads cocked and ready. I got hit, the scene was bad, my gurney was drenched it looked like a c- section took place with all the bloody rags. I was in my bag, it only takes me one time to learn, I learnt, that's what led up to me carrying twins with extra mags. Who wants it? All I needed was a sign and I'll make sure Nikkas knew why I man the frontline. I had nothing to lose. If it wasn't for my homie edgar I'll be dead in this six sextillion ton freezer, kept Teflon's because they're Kevlar eaters, muscle burners and bone breakers ya know... problem solvers. If homies came at me, when the smoke clears somebody's block gonna be chipping in to cop rip tees. When the streets make attempts on your life it changes you, when the streets kill your homies it changes you even more, I became prone to violence so as soon as I walked out my project door I was ready for war, duce duces, quarters, trey 8's, understanding build ciphers, three five sevens, nines, forty fours and forty fives for the summer, Mac tens, elevens and choppers hung over my shoulder to be discreet in colder weather. Where I'm from in the slums all year round is killing season, if ya wasn't prepared to defend when dudes was squeez'n, you'll be a stiff body leak'n a few minutes after you stop breath'n.

Eliza Segiet

Eliza Segioet

Eliza Segiet - A graduate of Jagiellonian University, The author of poetry volumes. *Romans z sobą* [*Romance with Oneself*] (2013), *Myślne miraże* [*Mental Mirages*](2014), *Chmurność* [*Cloudiness*] (2016), *Magnetyczni* (2018) *Magnetic People*- translation published in The USA in 2018, *Nieparzyści* [*Unpaired*] (2019), A monodrama *Prześwity* [*Clearance*] (2015), a farce *Tandem* [*Tandem*] (2017), Mini novel *Bezgłośni* [*Voiceless*](2019). Her poems can be found in numerous anthologies both in Poland and abroad. She is a member of The Association of Polish Writers and The World Nations Writers Union. The laureate of The International Annual Publication of 2017 for the poem Questions, and for the Sea of Mist in Spillwords Press in 2018. For her volume of Magnetic People she won a literary award of a Golden Rose named after Jaroslaw Zielinski (Poland 2019 r.). Her poem The *Sea of Mists* was chosen as one of the best amidst the hundred best poems of 2018 by International Poetry Press Publication Canada. In The 2019 Poet's Yearbook, as the author of *Sea of Mists*, she was awarded with the prestigious Elite Writer's Status Award as one of the best poets of 2019 (July 2019).

She was awarded *World Poetic Star Award* by World Nations Writers Union – the world's largest Writers' Union from Kazakhstan (August 2019).

In September 2019 she was 1st Place Laureate (Foreign Poetry category) – in Contest *Quando È la Vita ad Invitare* for poem *Be Yourself* (Italy).

Her poem *Order* from volume *Unpaired* was selected as one of the 100 best poems of 2019 in International Poetry Press Publications (Canada).

In November 2019 she is a nominee for Pushcart Prize.

Help

In memory of Henry Dunant
– Founder of the International Committee of the Red Cross

Drawn close to evil
every day,
he found
more and more good
in himself.

He couldn't pass by
human wrongs
indifferently.
He helped because
he saw and knew better
– when someone needs help –
they must experience it.

Sick or wounded,
brother or foe,
for him they were

Human.

translated by Artur Komoter

Harmony

In memory of Frédéric Passy
- Founder and President of the first French peace association (Société française pour l'arbitrage entre nations)

He noticed
that for some,
natural disasters
mean more
than war drama.

He knew
that the human domain
should be
striving for harmony,

his goal was
– reconciliation between nations.

After all, peace
depends on reason
and action,

unpredictable
can be the elements.

translated by Artur Komoter

Faith

I saw death.
A man did not die,
but the faith in him.

I saw a fall.
Yesterday of a man
– today of the people.

Elements
are not our work.

We create hatred,
– which kills.

translated by Artur Komoter

William S. Peters Sr.

Bill's writing career spans a period of over 50 years. Being first Published in 1972, Bill has since went on to Author in excess of 50 additional Volumes of Poetry, Short Stories, etc., expressing his thoughts on matters of the Heart, Spirit, Consciousness and Humanity. His primary focus is that of Love, Peace and Understanding!

Bill says . . .

I have always likened Life to that of a Garden. So, for me, Life is simply about the Seeds we Sow and Nourish. All things we "Think and Do", will "Be" Cause and eventually manifest itself to being an "Effect" within our own personal "Existences" and "Experiences" . . . whether it be Fruit, Flowers, Weeds or Barren Landscapes! Bill highly regards the Fruits of his Labor and wishes that everyone would thus go on to plant "Lovely" Seeds on "Good Ground" in their own Gardens of Life!

to connect with Bill, he is all things Inner Child

www.iaminnerchild.com

Personal Web Site

www.iamjustbill.com

A poem for this day . . . and those to come

It was not until
I was assigned
To write a poem
About Jean Henry Dunant
&
Frédéric Passy
That I became keenly aware
Of who they were

So I beg your indulgence,
For my offering
May not be much of a poem,
But most certainly
Their lives were . . .
And still are!

You see,
Somewhere within their psyche,
Their dreams and beliefs
And their hopes
For a better way,
They were inspired
To create,
Just as they have done for me, here
As I attempt to
Share with you
A bit about
Who they are,
And how they continue
To affect you & i

Jean Henry Dunant
Saw a red cross
As a symbol

And thus brought it to life
For the purposes
Of aiding those
Who were in need . . .
Yes, he like, perhaps you an i
Was driven
To see his vision . . .
work! . . . where as
Frédéric Passy
Was not passé'
In the least
For he believed
That peace was
Something
We all deserved

He joined leagues
With others such as himself
And the 'League of Peace"
Was borne

So in conclusion
To avoid any confusion
My poem may offer,
Read through this volume
And visit the offered links
In the front of the book
To learn more . .
I implore you
to do so . . .
As I am . ..

Stay tuned, for each month
We all shall learn something
About some of the . . .
Recipients of
The Nobel Peace Prizes

Monsters in the Garden

There are monsters lurking
In our once pristine gardens
Of civility,
Tolerance and acceptance

There is a hole
In the bottom of the bowl
Of compassion,
So we find great self favor
As we exercise our inhumane flavor
When lashing out at others
Who are different ...
Well aren't we all?

Who stands tall these days,
Save edifices and buildings
Of our erroneous deceit

The repleteness
Of our incompleteness
Is astounding
As we as a humanity
Are floundering
In our own soured regurgitations
Of the soured meals of persuasion
We have ingested
Occasion after occasion
That can not be digested

I must confess,
Yes I must,
For I too have violated
The trust
Of which we have been
Endowed with

As we shift from the 'enough'
To wanting more
Than our needs

The seeds of malcontent
Have been spent
All over the place,
Regardless of our fears
Of the morrow
Or the tear filled sorrows
Of our ludicrous
Self induced lament

These monsters,
The monsters
Who lurk in the shadows
In our holy gardens
Are none other
Than ourselves

Monsters in the Garden

Desire

Take not that which you dislike,
Nor that which you do not want
Into the
New Day,
New Year

"Today is the first day of the rest of your life",
As is tomorrow,
The next day,
And the next

Do not waste nor squander
Your opportunity,
our opportunity
For change,
A change for the better

It is your choice,
your voice,
Your choice"
To be that which you desire . . .
What do you desire ?

Though we may never forget,
We can forgive . . .
Forgive others . . .
Forgive your self,
And let your joyful expectations
And intent
Be met . . .
This NEW DAY,
This NEW YEAR
By your greater self!

What do you desire?

January
2020
Featured Poets

~ * ~

B S Tyagi

Andy Scott

Ashok Chakravarthy Tholana

Anwer Ghani

i FLY
because I Can
...said the Dreamer to the world.
www.iamjustbill.com

B S
Tyagi

B S Tyagi

B S Tyagi comes from India. He writes in both Hindi and English. He has several books- fiction and non-fiction to his credit. His poems have been included in several anthologies. He writes short stories which regularly appear in national and international literary magazines. His write-ups and poems have appeared in national and international magazines. Besides, he has translated four books of poems. He shies away from public celebrations and prizes.

Light Of My Soul

After the wanderings of ages
Like the rudderless ship in the sea
Light of soul is seen over yonder
That appears a heartbeat away
Know not how to reach there
How to greet…
Words fail.
Heart leaps up at the spark
That ever draws me
And brims me over with joys
Tears blur my eyes
My soul aches and flutters
With longing to take flight…
And vanish on the horizon
Bravo! My last but best efforts
To mingle with…
Sans footprints on the sands of Time.

Oh The Times!

Oh the times!
Pollution is abroad
No speech is unadulterated
No relation is pure
Feelings are trodden upon
Values messed up.
Actions no more speak as loud as words
Hearts seldom beat for others
Selfishness overrides man
Doubts crawl into inner sanctum
Where have we arrived?

Word...

Word is *Brahman*
It emerged from *Hiranyagarbh*
And wandered in the ether
Man's heart vibrated
He heard its rapturous melody
Swayed in ecstasy
And lost in sacred silence.
The other day...
The predator pounced upon the word
And preserved the kill
A dictionary is compiled
It hardly objected
But, was it at ease?
Lexicons continue multiplying
Then words, words, words
Words sans soul!

Andy
Scott

Andy Scott

Andrew Scott is a native of Fredericton, NB. During his time as an active poet, Andrew Scott has taken the time to speak in front of a classrooms, judge poetry competitions as well as be published worldwide in such publications as The Art of Being Human, Battered Shadows and The Broken Ones. His books, Snake With A Flower, The Phoenix Has Risen, The Path, The Storm Is Coming and Through My Eyes are available now. Searching is his fifth poetry collection.

To contact Andrew, email ...andrewscott.scott@gmail.com
http://twitter.com/JustMaritimeBoy
http://andrewmscott.com
http://www.facebook.com/andymscott
http://www.facebook.com/JustaMaritimeBoy

Waterloo Avenue

This place used to be full of activity.
Family gatherings all through the week.
Streets full of children playing their games.
Cheering laughter filled the air.

The downward spiral of life
happened so slow here
in this old, rotting place
of the homes that are falling
one by one into the ground.

It was not an industry
that collapsed this place.
It was decades of loneliness
that cracked the sidewalks.

The strong pillars crumbled,
people and families moved
and the homes were too big,
expensive to find new owners.
Weeds overtook the lawns
and grew over the regal look.

Fresh, vibrant paint
frayed, peeled away with age.
Wood split all along
the sides that were there to protect.
Leaving the homes open to all.

Animals crawling in the night
have overtaken the avenue,
making the once prestigious
a shelter for the beaten.

The generations before,
that built and lived here,
must now be crying spirits.
Seeing what they built
falling more and more each year.

Waterloo Avenue crumbling
into a beaten land
to know one's fault but their own.

This Old Tractor

This old tractor has been with me
for every morning, starting at five,
without fail for thirty four years.

The fields and crops may have failed
due to the weather or soil not cooperating
but this old tractor tills it perfectly.
A lot straighter that the horses used before.

The thoughts and plans made
from this squeaky seat.
All made just as the sun
was making this old farm glow.

Beads of rust have covered
this piece of machinery.
Believe it adds to the character.
I still purrs like a kitten
and has never failed
in giving an honest day's work.

As long as this farm is working,
the farms hands may come and go,
but this comforting old, rusty tractor
will always be with me.

Esmeralda's Eyes (Villanelle)

Do not look into Esmeralda's Eyes
you will believe they are heaven sent
Will be hypnotized by the lies

giving away all emotional ties
to the new, heartless present
Do not look into Esmeralda's Eyes

pieces of the soul dies
lifeless, taken without consent
Will be hypnotized by the lies

no one sympathizes with your cries
in softness you are spent
Do not look into Esmeralda's Eyes

she will never apologize
about where you went
Will be hypnotized by the lies

the pain is a tried and true exercise
that has no heart left to repent
Do not look into Esmeralda's Eyes
Will be hypnotized by the lies

Andy Scott

Ashok Chakravarthy Tholana

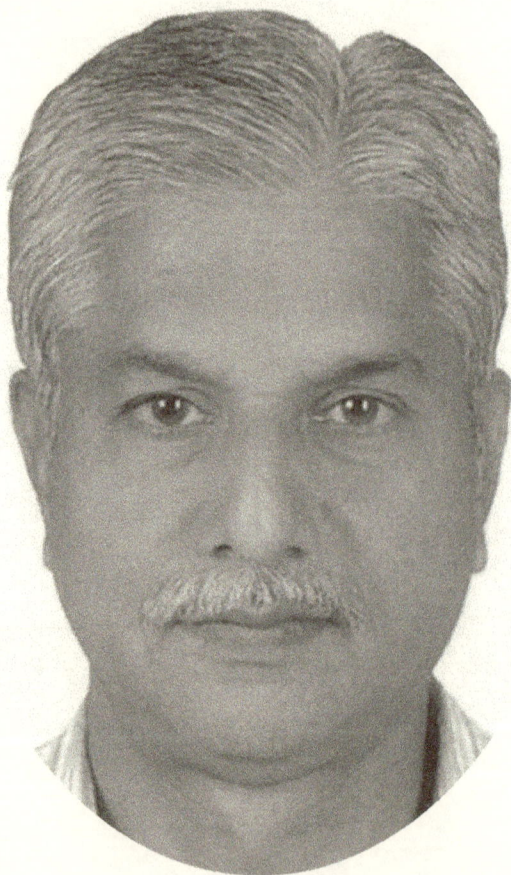

A poet-writer-reviewer, Dr. Ashok Chakravarthy Tholana hails from Hyderabad City, T-State, INDIA. During his 30-year poetry stint, his poems got published in no less than 90 countries. He was conferred with several prestigious national and international awards that include four Doctorates and quite a lot of prestigious laurels, commendations and titles. His poetry is aimed at promoting Universal Brotherhood and Peace, Protection of Environment & Nature, Safeguarding Children's and Human Rights etc. Out of 18 volumes of English poetry, 7 have been published so far. Dr. Ashok received commendations from former President and Prime Minister, India, Queen Elizabeth of Britain, Princess of Wales, President of France, Prime Minister of Switzerland, UNO, UNESCO, UNICEF etc.

Eternal Delights

The world is a mere decoration of delusions
Yet, we vie for them without future visions;
Fleeting pleasures are sheer wombs of grief
Realize, they play havoc in our day-to-day life.

Selfish world supports the notion of supremacy
Conflicts and wars control the law of diplomacy,
Every continent is torn between conflicts and ruin
Midnight peace has become scarce for humans.

Every heart longs for a life of peace and amity
Every heart aspires to live in a place of serenity;
But for a living, why we indulge in aimless actions?
And get perturbed, yes, with self-inflicted pains.

Desperate thoughts, often into the past roll back
Unaware, we ruffle the pages of childhood book,
The crescent moon, the twinkling stars appear,
We traverse the peace space in moon's glitter.

A positive approach with a wisdom-laced vision
Ushers a new dawn with peace and realization;
Be it the dawn, mid-day, dusk fall or mid-night
Only peace fills every heart with eternal delights.

The Beggar On The Street Lane

Everyone shun his dismal stature
As if he's not a human by nature
Forlorn, he stares into the void skies
With deep sunk tear-filled eyes;
Bone sucked and almost lifeless
Yet, he tries to move on, pitiless.
His tattered clothes, feeble body
Seems a dust-laden lifeless body
At times, street dogs hound him
At times, children too taunt him
If fate is so cruel towards a human
What's our concern for a co-human?
Caught in the vortex of illusions
Veiled by ignorance and possessions,
They incite us with fleeing a nuisance
To ignore the bond of care and concern.
But, the beggar on the street lane
Imparts to one and all, a fitting lesson
To rid ourselves from selfish motives
Lest, never can we realize life's objective.

Those Were The Days

Those were the days to cherish
Memories of childhood appear afresh,
Those playful and fun-filled days,
Those delight-filled schooling days,
Quite often in my thoughts, they flourish.

Those were the days to cherish
When teenage, unaware did vanish
Parental love and friendship I adored
Love was something, I deeply stored
Quite often in thoughts, they flourish.

Those were the days to cherish
When love encircled my heart's crush
The one I longed to be a life partner
Became a real dream in my love-empire
Quite often in thoughts, they flourish.

Those were the days to cherish
Life's upheavals appear and perish
The loss of parents, I could not digest
Even now, at times I feel totally lost
Quite often in thoughts, they flourish.

Those were the days to cherish, yes
Good or bad, dejected or full of bliss
The bygone age and the eclipsing past
In everyone; they leave a lasting impact
Quite often in thoughts, they flourish, yes.

Anwer
Ghani

Anwer Ghani is an award winner poet from Iraq. He was born in 1973 in Babylon. His name has appeared in more than fifty literary magazines and twenty anthologies in USA, UK and Asia and he has won many prizes; one of them is the "World Laureate-Best Poet in 2017 from WNWU". In 2018 he was nominated to Adelaide Award for poetry and in 2019 he is the winner of Rock Pebbles Literary Award and the award of United Spirit of Writers Academy for Poetry. Anwer is a religious scholar and consultant nephrologist and the author of more than eighty books; thirteenth of them are in English like; "Narratolyric writing"; (2016),"Antipoetic Poems";(2017) and "Mosaicked Poems"; (2018), and "The Styles of Poetry"; 2019.

https://www.facebook.com/anwerghani73

http://www.innerchildpress.com/anwer-ghani.php

The Fake Man

Please do not look at me or try to hear my voice. I'm sure you will not see anything and you will not hear anything because I'm just a fake man. I think you may want to find an idea in my mind; even a simple idea, but you should know that there is no thought in the mind of a fake man. You may expect to find a heart here, in my chest, but believe me you will find no heart here, in my chest, because I am just a fake man. My smile, my sad smile; it's a very fake smile. Our river, our dry river; it's fake like me. Dear friend, have you heard about my dreams? Yes, pink dreams, they are false dreams like my soul. Have you heard about my flower? Yes, romantic morning flower, is also a fake flower. Have you heard about my love? Yes my crazy love, it's also a fake love, because I'm a fake man.

The Fake Land

There are no rivers, no flowers, no fields in the false land. Everything is fake in the fake land even moon, even me; the fake story coming from mirage. These words, are fake words because they are shades of fake land. There are no sands in the fake land because the thief stole them on a sunny day. Oh, sorry, I forgot, no thief here in the fake land, nor the sun or the rivers. There is nothing in the fake land except false images. I mean very fake images. Our houses are fake, our fields are fake, our chickens are fake, and our faces are fake. Everything is fake here in a the fake land.

The Fake Time

I live without time, not because I am a gypsy thing but the truth is that my time is fake, I mean very fake. Yes I am the son of the fake time, full of fake mornings, fake evenings, fake days and fake nights. My breath, which enumirates the false moments, does not come out of my chest, it just plays as a strange bird. And the twilight that have long dreamed of the vehicle of love and nostalgya is not a real color, but just a fake brwon tale. I can tell you all fake promises, fake justifications and violations in the name of fake titles. I can tell you of injustice based on false justice because I am the son of the false time.

Remembering

our fallen soldiers of verse

Janet Perkins Caldwell
February 14, 1959 ~ September 20, 2016

Alan W. Jankowski
16 March 1961 ~ 10 March 2017

Coming
April 2020

The
World Healing, World Peace
International Poetry Symposium

Stay Tuned

for more information
intouch@innerchildpress.com
'building bridges of cultural understanding'
www.innerchildpress.com

Inner Child Press

News

Poetry Posse Members

We are so excited to share and announce a few of the current books, as well as the new and upcoming books of some of our Poetry Posse authors.

On the following pages we present to you ...

Jackie Davis Allen

Gail Weston Shazor

hülya n. yılmaz

Nizar Sartawi

Faleeha Hassan

Fahredin Shehu

Caroline 'Ceri' Nazareno

Eliza Segiet

William S. Peters, Sr.

Coming January 2020
www.innerchildpress.com

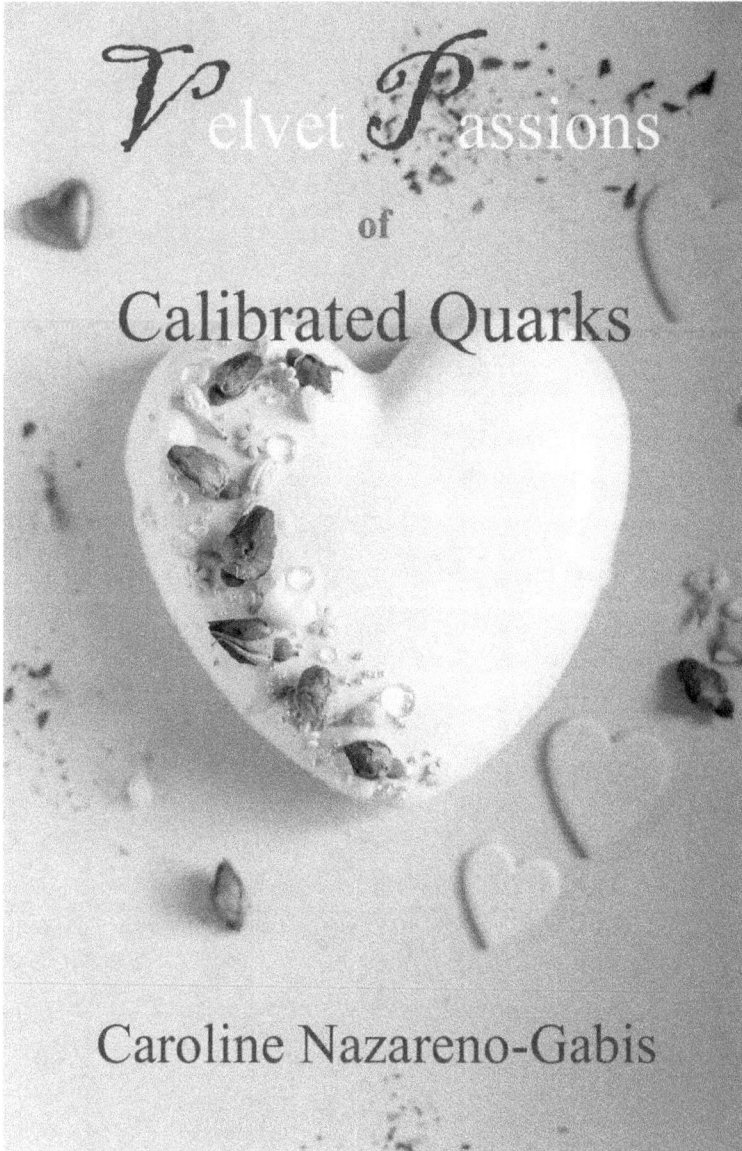

Velvet Passions

of

Calibrated Quarks

Caroline Nazareno-Gabis

Now Available

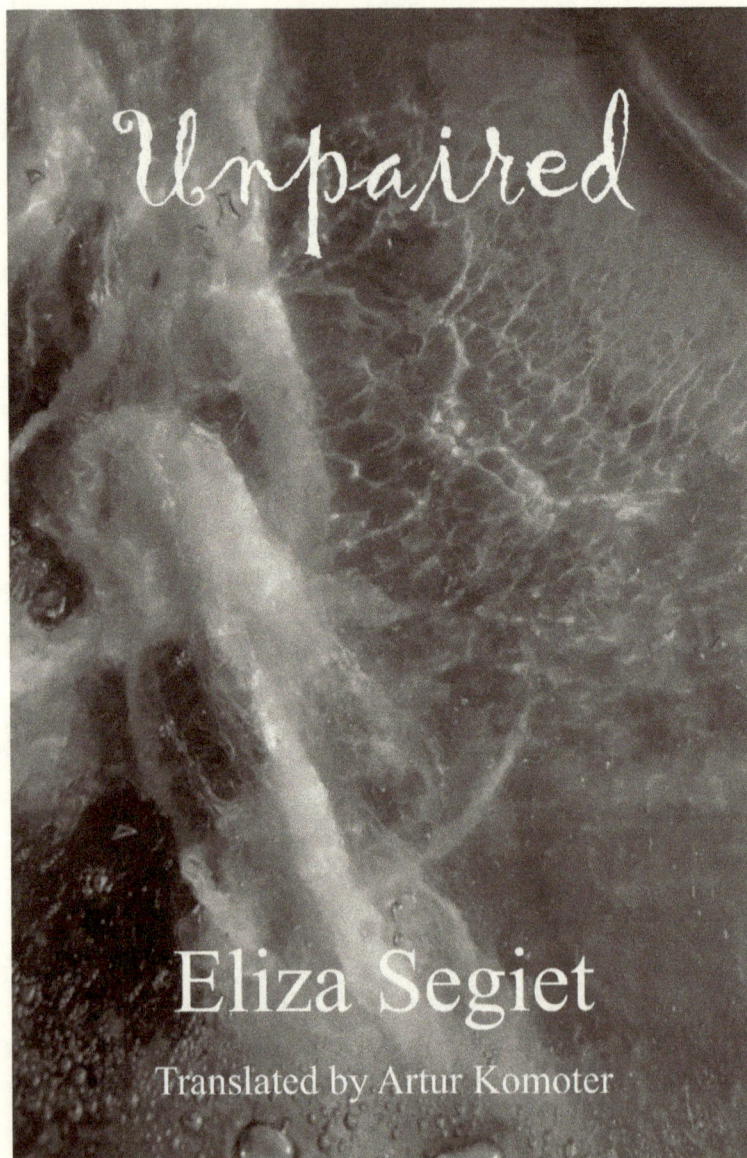

Unpaired

Eliza Segiet

Translated by Artur Komoter

Private Issue
www.innerchildpress.com

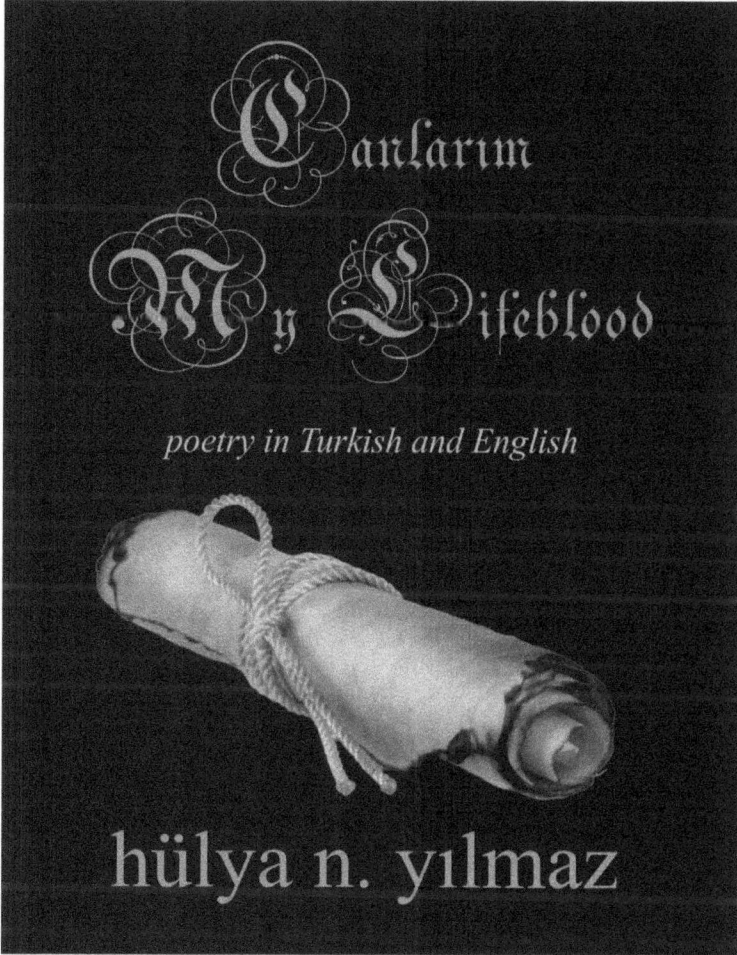

Canlarım

My Lifeblood

poetry in Turkish and English

hülya n. yılmaz

Coming January 2020
www.innerchildpress.com

Butterfly's Voice

Faleeha Hassan

Translated by William M. Hutchins

Now Available at
www.innerchildpress.com

No Illusions

Through the Looking Glass

Jackie Davis Allen

Inner Child Press News

Now Available at
www.innerchildpress.com

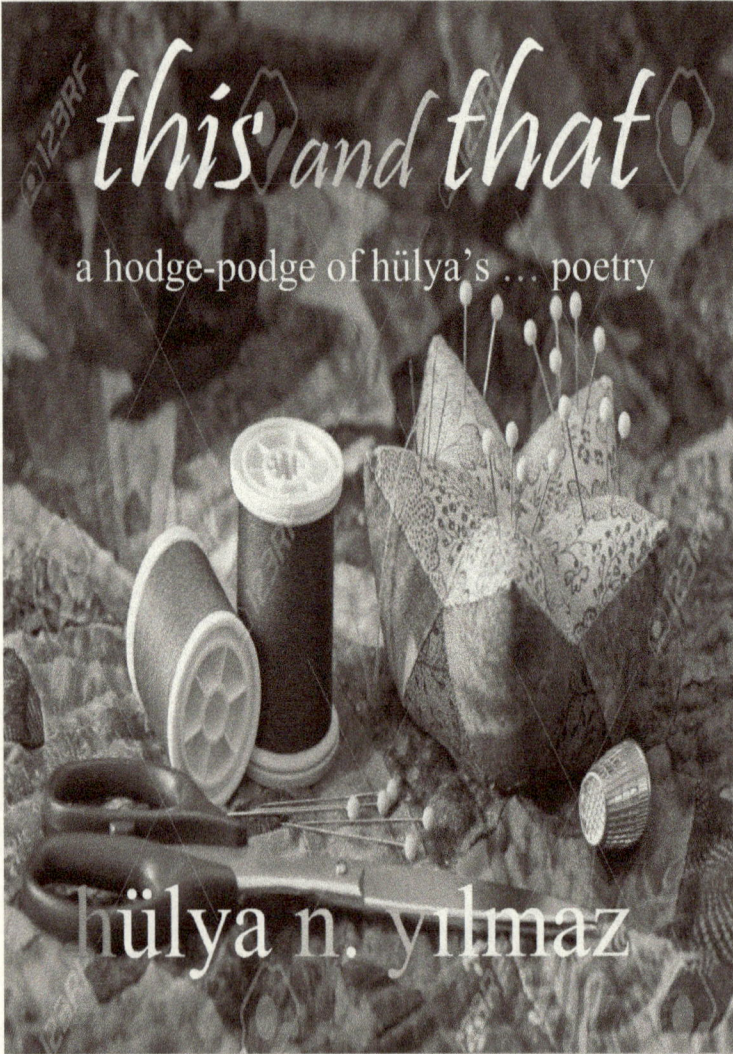

this *and* that

a hodge-podge of hülya's ... poetry

hülya n. yılmaz

Now Available at
www.innerchildpress.com

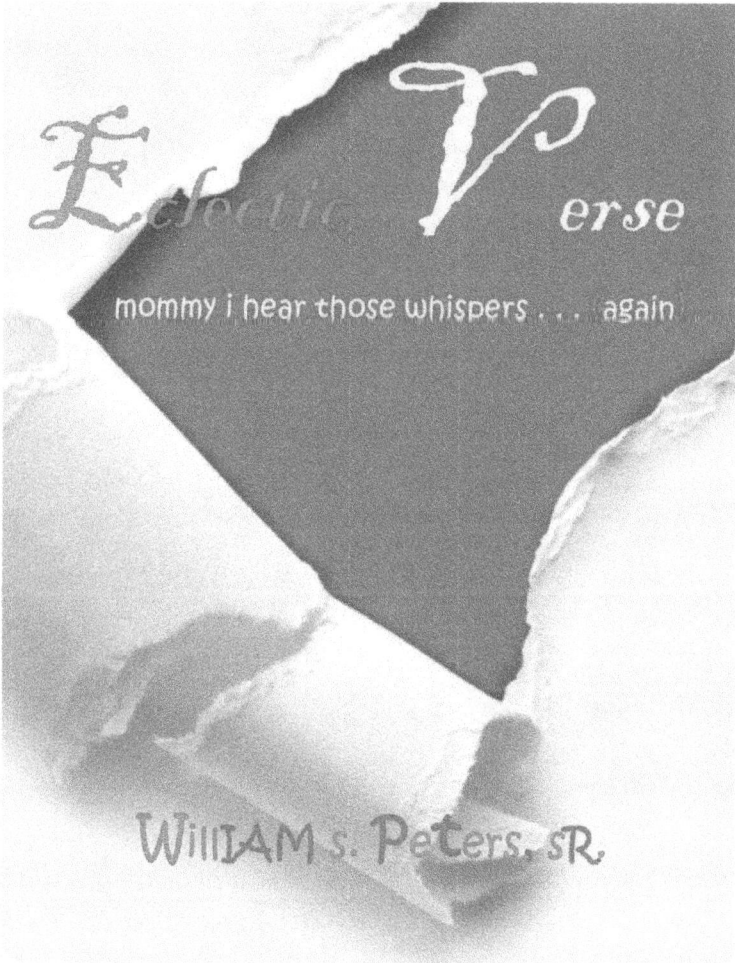

Inner Child Press News

Now Available at
www.innerchildpress.com

HERENOW

◆

FAHREDIN SHEHU

146

Now Available at

www.innerchildpress.com

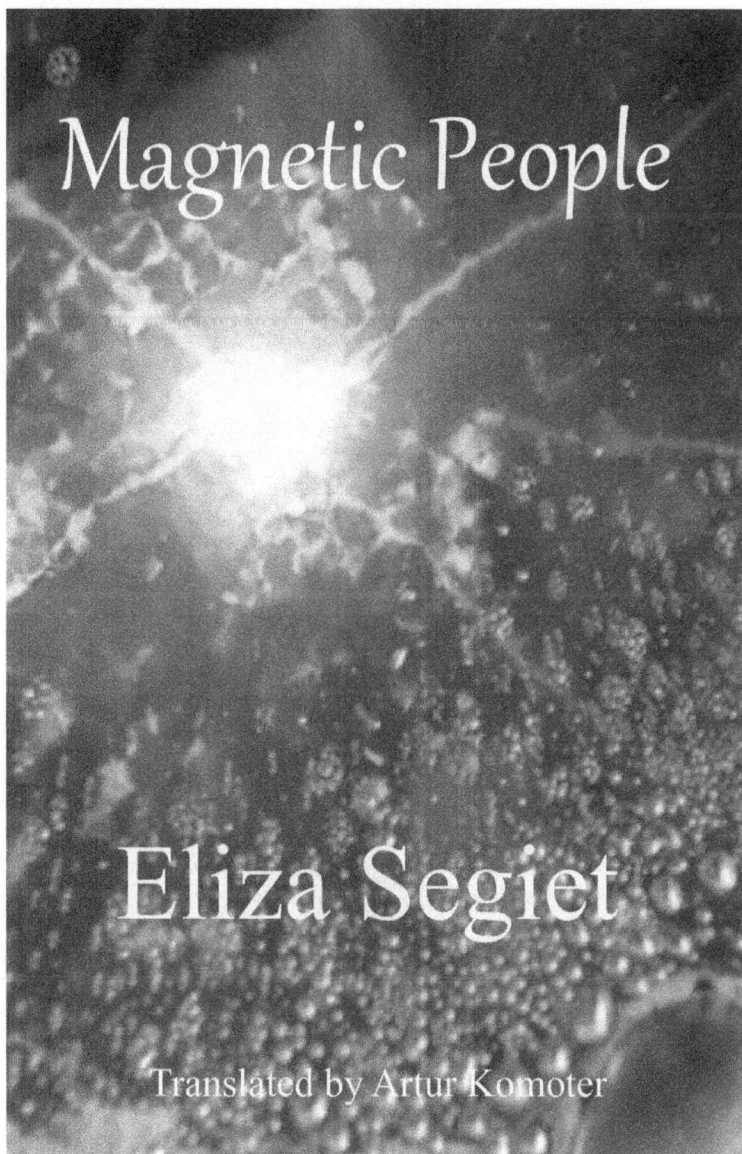

Now Available at
www.innerchildpress.com

Dark Side

of the

Moon

Jackie Davis Allen

Now Available at
www.innerchildpress.com

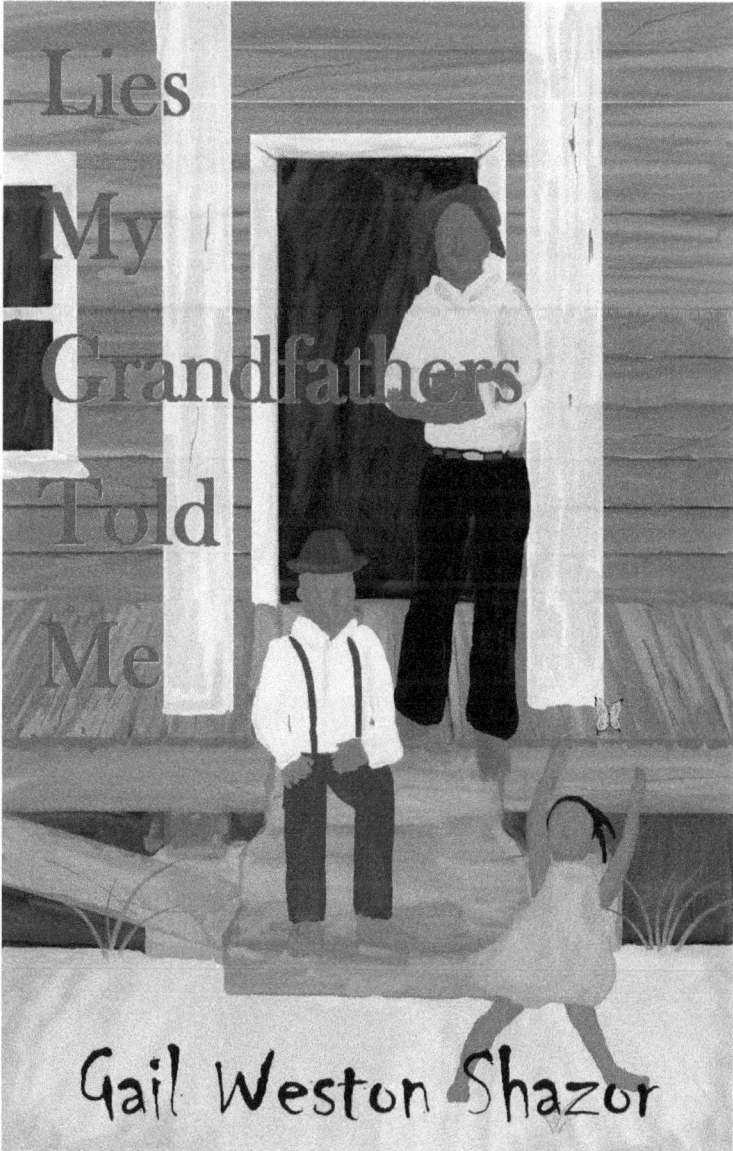

Lies My Grandfathers Told Me

Gail Weston Shazor

Inner Child Press News

Now Available at
www.innerchildpress.com

Aflame

Memoirs in Verse

hülya n. yılmaz

Now Available at
www.innerchildpress.com

My Shadow

Nizar Sartawi

Now Available at
www.innerchildpress.com

Now Available at
<u>www.innerchildpress.com</u>

Breakfast

for

Butterflies

Faleeha Hassan

Now Available at
www.innerchildpress.com

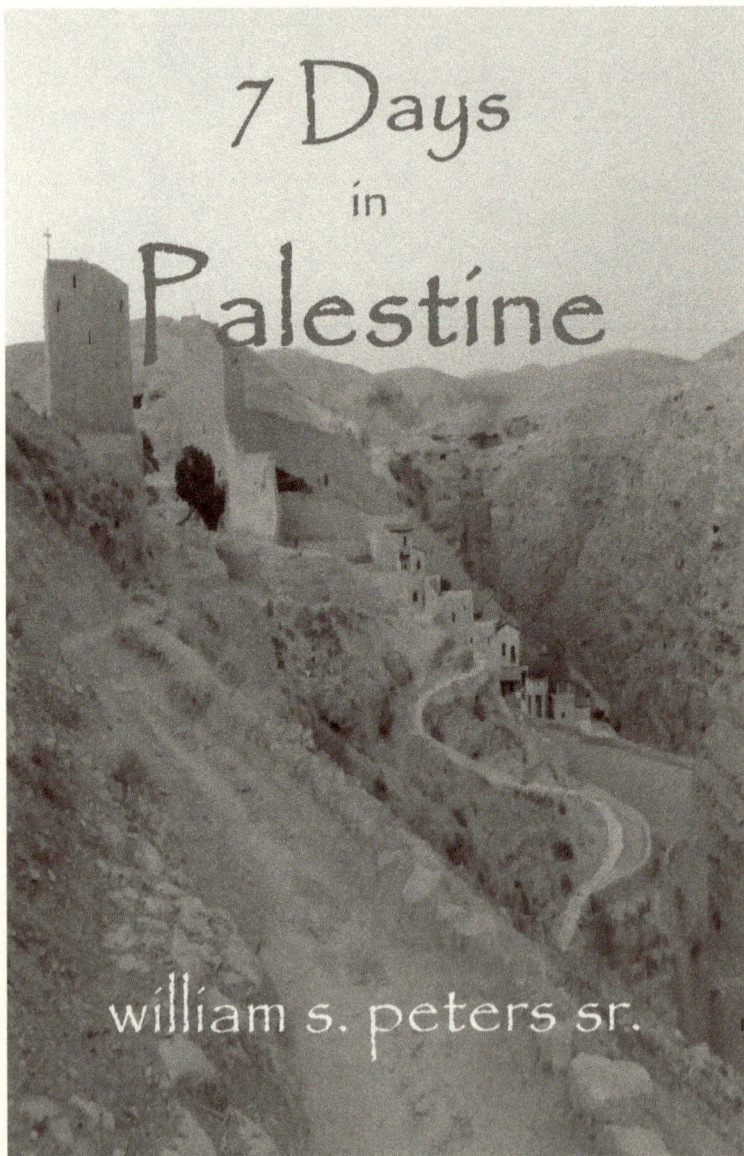

7 Days
in
Palestine

william s. peters sr.

Now Available at
www.innerchildpress.com

inner child press
presents

Tunisia My Love

william s. peters, sr.

Coming in the Summer of 2020

The Journey

Footprints and Shadows

Kosovo
Tunisia
Macedonia
Morocco
Jordan
Palestine
Israel
Italy
Turkey

a collection of poetry inspired during my travels

william s. peters, sr.

Now Available at
www.innerchildpress.com

Now Available at
www.innerchildpress.com

Now Available at
www.innerchildpress.com

Inward Reflections

Think on These Things
Book II

william s. peters, sr.

Now Available at
www.innerchildpress.com

Poetry
from the
Balkans

The Balkan Poets

Other

Anthological

works from

Inner Child Press International

www.innerchildpress.com

World Healing World Peace
2020

Poets for Humanity

Coming April 2020

www.worldhealingworldpeacepoetry.com

Inner Child Press International
presents

A Love Anthology
2019

The Love Poets

Now Available

www.worldhealingworldpeacepoetry.com

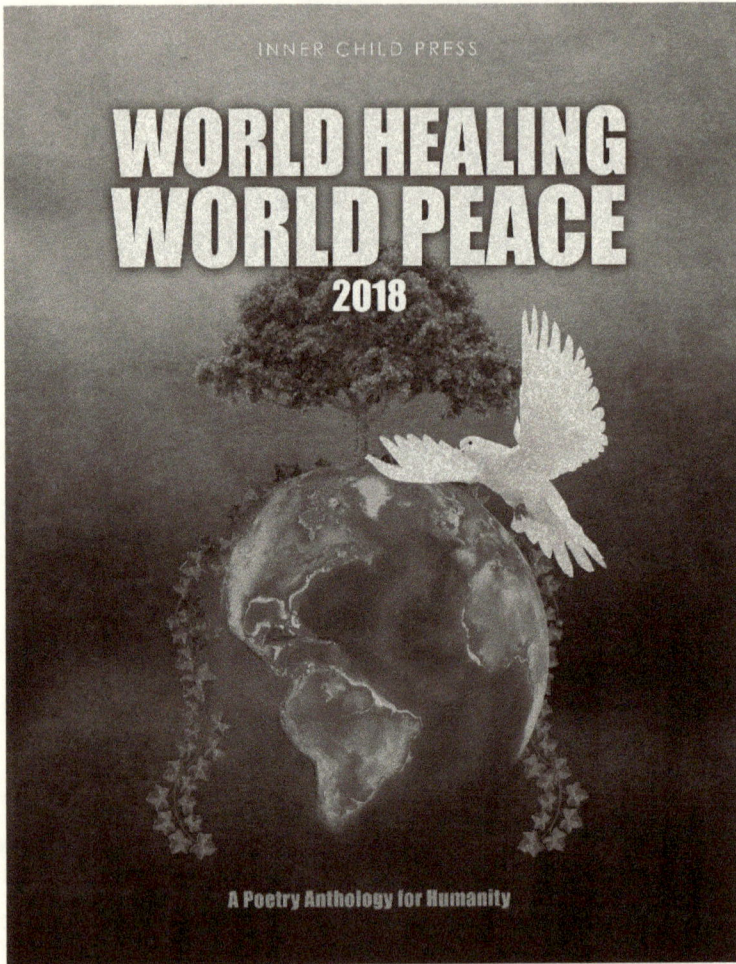

INNER CHILD PRESS

WORLD HEALING WORLD PEACE
2018

A Poetry Anthology for Humanity

Now Available

www.worldhealingworldpeacepoetry.com

Now Available

Now Available

www.innerchildpress.com/anthologies

healing through words

Poetry ... Prose ... Prayer ... Stories

a
Poetically
Spoken
Anthology
volume I
Collector's Edition

The Poetry Posse
Presents

an anthology
of

Love

The Poetry Posse 2016

Now Available

www.innerchildpress.com/anthologies

171

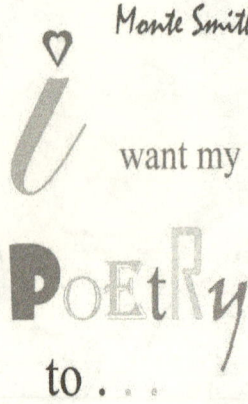

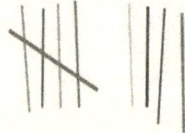

Now Available

www.innerchildpress.com/anthologies

The Year of the Poet
January 2014

The Poetry Posse

Jamie Bond
Gail Weston Shazor
Albert 'Infinite' Carrasco
Siddartha Beth Pierce
Janet P. Caldwell
June 'Bugg' Barefield
Debbie M. Allen
Tony Henninger
Joe DaVerbal Minddancer
Robert Gibbons
Neetu Wali
Shareef Abdur-Rasheed
William S. Peters, Sr.

Carnation

Our January Feature
Terri L. Johnson

the Year of the Poet
February 2014

violets

The Poetry Posse

Jamie Bond
Gail Weston Shazor
Albert 'Infinite' Carrasco
Siddartha Beth Pierce
Janet P. Caldwell
June 'Bugg' Barefield
Debbie M. Allen
Tony Henninger
Joe DaVerbal Minddancer
Robert Gibbons
Neetu Wali
Shareef Abdur-Rasheed
William S. Peters Sr.

Our February Features
Teresa E. Gallion & Robert Gibson

the Year of the Poet
March 2014

The Poetry Posse

Jamie Bond
Gail Weston Shazor
Albert 'Infinite' Carrasco
Siddartha Beth Pierce
Janet P. Caldwell
June 'Bugg' Barefield
Debbie M. Allen
Tony Henninger
Joe DaVerbal Minddancer
Robert Gibbons
Neetu Wali
Kimberly Burnham
William S. Peters. Sr.

daffodil

Our March Featured Poets
AliciaC. Cooper & hülya yılmaz

the Year of the Poet
April 2014

The Poetry Posse

Jamie Bond
Gail Weston Shazor
Albert 'Infinite' Carrasco
Siddartha Beth Pierce
Janet P. Caldwell
June 'Bugg' Barefield
Debbie M. Allen
Tony Henninger
Joe DaVerbal Minddancer
Robert Gibbons
Neetu Wali
Shareef Abdur-Rasheed
Kimberly Burnham
William S. Peters, Sr.

Sweet Pea

Our April Featured Poets
Fahredin Shehu
Martina Reisz Newberry
Justin Blackburn
Monte Smith

celebrating international poetry month

Now Available

www.innerchildpress.com/the-year-of-the-poet

The Year of the Poet
September 2014

Aster   Morning-Glory

Wild Chicory of September Birth Your Flower

September Feature Poets
Florence Malone * Keith Alan Hamilton

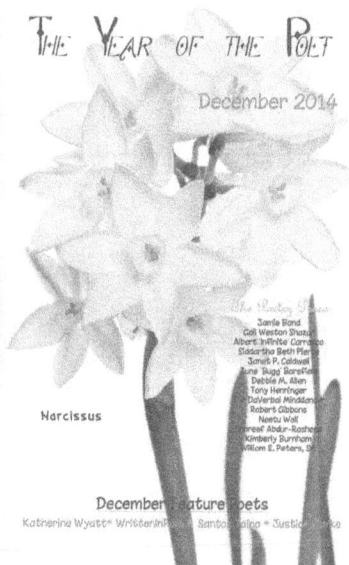

The Poetry Posse
Jamie Bond * Gail Weston Shazor * Albert 'Infinite' Carrasco * Siddartha Beth Pierce
Janet P. Caldwell * June 'Bugg' Barefield * Debbie M. Allen * Tony Henninger
Joe DaVerbal Minddancer * Robert Gibbons * Neetu Wali * Shareef Abdur-Rasheed
Kimberly Burnham * William S. Peters, Sr.

THE YEAR OF THE POET
October 2014

Red Poppy

The Poetry Posse
Jamie Bond * Gail Weston Shazor * Albert 'Infinite' Carrasco * Siddartha Beth Pierce
Janet P. Caldwell * June 'Bugg' Barefield * Debbie M. Allen * Tony Henninger
Joe DaVerbal Minddancer * Robert Gibbons * Neetu Wali * Shareef Abdur-Rasheed
Kimberly Burnham * William S. Peters, Sr.

October Feature Poets
Ceri Naz * Rajendra Padhi * Elizabeth Castillo

THE YEAR OF THE POET
November 2014

Chrysanthemum

The Poetry Posse
Jamie Bond * Gail Weston Shazor * Albert 'Infinite' Carrasco * Siddartha Beth Pierce
Janet P. Caldwell * June 'Bugg' Barefield * Debbie M. Allen * Tony Henninger
Joe DaVerbal Minddancer * Robert Gibbons * Neetu Wali * Shareef Abdur-Rasheed
Kimberly Burnham * William S. Peters, Sr.

November Feature Poets
Jocelyn Mosman * Jackie Allen * James Moore * Neville Hiatt

THE YEAR OF THE POET
December 2014

The Poetry Posse
Jamie Bond
Gail Weston Shazor
Albert 'Infinite' Carrasco
Siddartha Beth Pierce
Janet P. Caldwell
June 'Bugg' Barefield
Debbie M. Allen
Tony Henninger
DaVerbal Minddancer
Robert Gibbons
Neetu Wali
Shareef Abdur-Rasheed
Kimberly Burnham
William S. Peters, Sr.

Narcissus

December Feature Poets
Katherine Wyatt* WrittenInPeace * Santosh Bakaya * Justice Burke

Now Available

www.innerchildpress.com/the-year-of-the-poet

THE YEAR OF THE POET II
January 2015

Garnet

The Poetry Posse

Jamie Bond
Gail Weston Shazor
Albert 'Infinite' Carrasco
Siddartha Beth Pierce
Janet P. Caldwell
Tony Henninger
Joe DaVerbal Minddancer
Robert Gibbons
Neetu Wali
Shareef Abdur ~ Rasheed
Kimberly Burnham
Ann White
Keith Alan Hamilton
Katherine Wyatt
Fahredin Shehu
Hülya N. Yılmaz
Teresa E. Gallion
Jackie Allen
William S. Peters, Sr.

January Feature Poets
Bismay Mohanti * Jen Walls * Eric Judah

THE YEAR OF THE POET II
February 2015

Amethyst

THE POETRY POSSE

Jamie Bond
Gail Weston Shazor
Albert 'Infinite' Carrasco
Siddartha Beth Pierce
Janet P. Caldwell
Tony Henninger
Joe DaVerbal Minddancer
Robert Gibbons
Neetu Wali
Shareef Abdur ~ Rasheed
Kimberly Burnham
Ann White
Keith Alan Hamilton
Katherine Wyatt
Hülya N. Yılmaz
Teresa E. Gallion
Jackie Allen
William S. Peters, Sr.

FEBRUARY FEATURE POETS
Iram Fatima * Bob McNeil * Kerstin Centervall

The Year of the Poet II
March 2015

Our Featured Poets

Heung Sook * Anthony Arnold * Alicia Poland

Bloodstone

The Poetry Posse 2015
Jamie Bond * Gail Weston Shazor * Albert 'Infinite' Carrasco
Siddartha Beth Pierce * Janet P. Caldwell * Tony Henninger
Joe DaVerbal Minddancer * Neetu Wali * Shareef Abdur ~ Rasheed
Kimberly Burnham * Ann White * Keith Alan Hamilton
Katherine Wyatt * Fahredin Shehu * Hülya N. Yılmaz
Teresa E. Gallion * Jackie Allen * William S. Peters, Sr.

The Year of the Poet II
April 2015

Celebrating International Poetry Month

Our Featured Poets

Raja Williams * Dennis Ferado * Laure Charazac

Diamonds

The Poetry Posse 2015
Jamie Bond * Gail Weston Shazor * Albert 'Infinite' Carrasco
Siddartha Beth Pierce * Janet P. Caldwell * Tony Henninger
Joe DaVerbal Minddancer * Neetu Wali * Shareef Abshur ~ Rasheed
Kimberly Burnham * Ann White * Keith Alan Hamilton
Katherine Wyatt * Fahredin Shehu * Hülya N. Yılmaz
Teresa E. Gallion * Jackie Allen * William S. Peters, Sr.

Now Available

www.innerchildpress.com/the-year-of-the-poet

The Year of the Poet II
May 2015

May's Featured Poets

Geri Algeri
Akin Mosi Chinnery
Anna Jakubcza

Emeralds

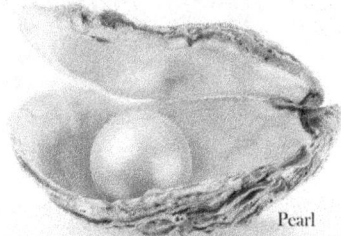

The Poetry Posse 2015
Jamie Bond * Gail Weston Shazor * Albert 'Infinite' Carrasco
Siddartha Beth Pierce * Janet P. Caldwell * Tony Henninger
Joe DaVerbal Minddancer * Neetu Wali * Shareef Abdur – Rasheed
Kimberly Burnham * Ann White * Keith Alan Hamilton
Katherine Wyatt * Fahredin Shehu * Hülya N. Yılmaz
Teresa E. Gallion * Jackie Allen * William S. Peters, Sr.

The Year of the Poet II
June 2015

June's Featured Poets

Anahit Arustamyan * Yvette D. Murrell * Regina A. Walker

Pearl

The Poetry Posse 2015
Jamie Bond * Gail Weston Shazor * Albert 'Infinite' Carrasco
Siddartha Beth Pierce * Janet P. Caldwell * Tony Henninger
Joe DaVerbal Minddancer * Neetu Wali * Shareef Abdur – Rasheed
Kimberly Burnham * Ann White * Keith Alan Hamilton
Katherine Wyatt * Fahredin Shehu * Hülya N. Yılmaz
Teresa E. Gallion * Jackie Allen * William S. Peters, Sr.

The Year of the Poet II
July 2015

The Featured Poets for July 2015
Abhik Shome * Christina Neal * Robert Neal

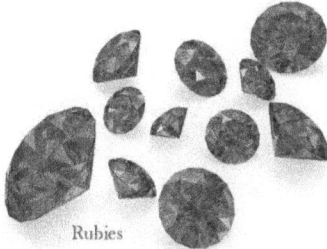

Rubies

The Poetry Posse 2015
Jamie Bond * Gail Weston Shazor * Albert 'Infinite' Carrasco
Siddartha Beth Pierce * Janet P. Caldwell * Tony Henninger
Joe DaVerbal Minddancer * Neetu Wali * Shareef Abdur – Rasheed
Kimberly Burnham * Ann White * Keith Alan Hamilton
Katherine Wyatt * Fahredin Shehu * Hülya N. Yılmaz
Teresa E. Gallion * Jackie Allen * William S. Peters, Sr.

The Year of the Poet II
August 2015

Peridot

Featured Poets
Gayle Howell
Ann Chalasz
Christopher Schultz

The Poetry Posse 2015
Jamie Bond * Gail Weston Shazor * Albert 'Infinite' Carrasco
Siddartha Beth Pierce * Janet P. Caldwell * Tony Henninger
Joe DaVerbal Minddancer * Neetu Wali * Shareef Abdur – Rasheed
Kimberly Burnham * Ann White * Keith Alan Hamilton
Katherine Wyatt * Fahredin Shehu * Hülya N. Yılmaz
Teresa E. Gallion * Jackie Allen * William S. Peters, Sr

Now Available

www.innerchildpress.com/the-year-of-the-poet

The Year of the Poet II
September 2015

Featured Poets

Alfreda Ghee ~ Lonneice Weeks Badley ~ Demetrios Trifiatis

Sapphires

The Poetry Posse 2015

Jamie Bond * Gail Weston Shazor * Albert 'Infinite' Carrasco
Siddartha Beth Pierce * Janet P. Caldwell * Tony Henninger
Joe DaVerbal Minddancer * Neetu Wali * Shareef Abdur – Rasheed
Kimberly Burnham * Ann White * Keith Alan Hamilton
Katherine Wyatt * Fahredin Shehu * Hülya N. Yılmaz
Teresa E. Gallion * Jackie Allen * William S. Peters. Sr.

The Year of the Poet II
October 2015

Featured Poets

Monte Smith * Laura J. Wolfe * William Washington

Opal

The Poetry Posse 2015

Jamie Bond * Gail Weston Shazor * Albert 'Infinite' Carrasco
Siddartha Beth Pierce * Janet P. Caldwell * Tony Henninger
Joe DaVerbal Minddancer * Neetu Wali * Shareef Abdur – Rasheed
Kimberly Burnham * Ann White * Keith Alan Hamilton
Katherine Wyatt * Fahredin Shehu * Hülya N. Yılmaz
Teresa E. Gallion * Jackie Allen * William S. Peters. Sr.

The Year of the Poet II
November 2015

Featured Poets

Alan W. Jankowski
Bismay Mohanty
James Moore

Topaz

The Poetry Posse 2015

Jamie Bond * Gail Weston Shazor * Albert 'Infinite' Carrasco
Siddartha Beth Pierce * Janet P. Caldwell * Tony Henninger
Joe DaVerbal Minddancer * Neetu Wali * Shareef Abdur – Rasheed
Kimberly Burnham * Ann White * Keith Alan Hamilton
Katherine Wyatt * Fahredin Shehu * Hülya N. Yılmaz
Teresa E. Gallion * Jackie Allen * William S. Peters. Sr.

The Year of the Poet II
December 2015

Featured Poets

Kerione Bryan * Michelle Joan Barulich * Neville Hiatt

Turquoise

The Poetry Posse 2015

Jamie Bond * Gail Weston Shazor * Albert 'Infinite' Carrasco
Siddartha Beth Pierce * Janet P. Caldwell * Tony Henninger
Joe DaVerbal Minddancer * Neetu Wali * Shareef Abdur – Rasheed
Kimberly Burnham * Ann White * Keith Alan Hamilton
Katherine Wyatt * Fahredin Shehu * Hülya N. Yılmaz
Teresa E. Gallion * Jackie Allen * William S. Peters. Sr.

Now Available

www.innerchildpress.com/the-year-of-the-poet

The Year of the Poet III
January 2016

Featured Poets
Lana Joseph * Atom Cyrus Rush * Christena Williams

Dark-eyed Junco

The Poetry Posse 2016

The Year of the Poet III
February 2016

Featured Poets
Anthony Arnold
Anna Chalasz
Andre Haydenshe

Puffin

The Poetry Posse 2016

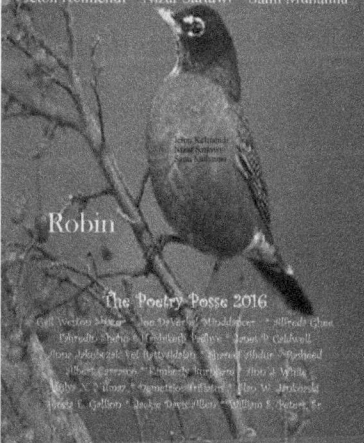

The Year of the Poet
March 2016
Featured Poets
Jeton Kelmendi   Nizar Sartawi   Sami Muhanna

Robin

The Poetry Posse 2016

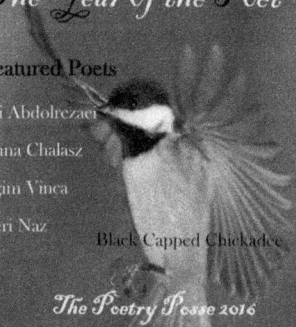

The Year of the Poet III

Featured Poets

Ali Abdolrezaei

Anna Chalasz

Agim Vinca

Ceri Naz

Black Capped Chickadee

The Poetry Posse 2016

celebrating international poetry month

Now Available

www.innerchildpress.com/the-year-of-the-poet

The Year of the Poet
May 2016

Bob Strum
Barbara Allan
D.L. Davis

Oriole

The Year of the Poet III
June 2016

Featured Poets

Qibrije Demiri- Frangu
Naime Beqiraj
Faleeha Hassan
Bedri Zyberaj

Black Necked Silt

The Poetry Posse 2016

The Year of the Poet
July

Iram Fatima 'Ashi'
Langley Shazor
Jody Doty
Emilia T. Davis

Indigo Bunting

The Poetry Posse 2016

The Year of the Poet III
August 2016

Featured Poets

Anita Dash
Irena Jovanovic
Malgorzata Gouluda

Painted Bunting

The Poetry Posse 2016

Now Available

www.innerchildpress.com/the-year-of-the-poet

The Year of the Poet III
September 2016

Featured Poets

Simone Weber
Abhijit Sen
Eunice Barbara C. Novio

Long Billed Curlew

The Poetry Posse 2016

The Year of the Poet III
October 2016

Featured Poets

Lana Joseph
Krishnamurthy
Janet Moore

Barn Owl

The Poetry Posse 2016

The Year of the Poet III
November 2016

Featured Poets

Rosemary Burns
Robin Ouzman Hislop
Lonneice Weeks-Badler

Northern Cardinal

The Poetry Posse 2016

Gail Weston Shazor * Caroline Nazareno * Jen Walls
Nizar Sartawi * Janet P. Caldwell * Alfredo Ghou
Jon DeVerbal Mbaddacser * Shareef Abdur – Rasheed
Albert Carrasco * Kimberly Burnham * Elizabeth Castillo
Hülya N. Yılmaz * Demetrios Trifiatis * Alan W. Jankowski
Teresa E. Gallion * Jackie Davis Allen * William S. Peters, Sr.

The Year of the Poet III
December 2016

Featured Poets

Samih Masoud
Mountassir Aziz Bien
Abdulkadir Musa

Rough Legged Hawk

The Poetry Posse 2016

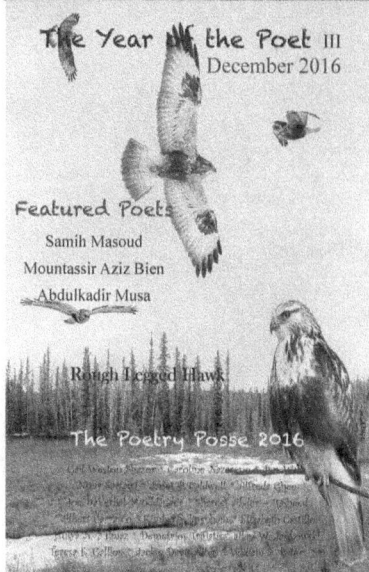

Now Available

www.innerchildpress.com/the-year-of-the-poet

Now Available

The Year of the Poet IV
May 2017

The Flowering Dogwood Tree

Featured Poets
Kallisa Powell
Alicja Maria Kuberska
Fethi Sassi

The Poetry Posse 2017

Gail Weston Shazor * Caroline Nazareno * Tejmoy Mohanty
Teresa E. Gallion * Anna Jakubczak Vel Ratty Adalan
Joe DaVerbal Minddancer * Shareef Abdur – Rasheed
Albert Carrasco * Kimberly Burnham * Elizabeth Castillo
Hülya N. Yılmaz * Pelasho Hassan * Jackie Davis Allen
Jan Wells * Nizar Sartawi * * William S. Peters, Sr.

The Year of the Poet IV
June 2017

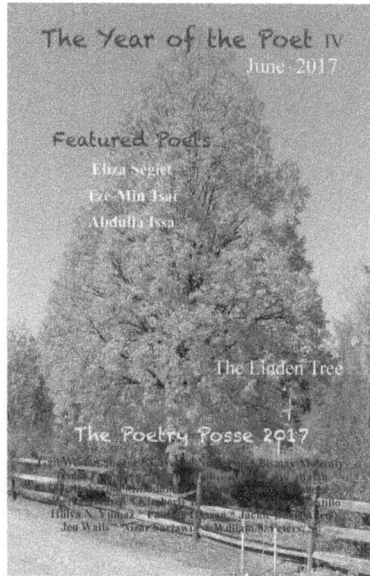

Featured Poets
Eliza Segiet
Tzu-Min Tsai
Abdulla Issa

The Linden Tree

The Poetry Posse 2017

Hülya N. Yılmaz * Pelasho Hassan * Jackie Davis Allen
Jan Wells * Nizar Sartawi * William S. Peters, Sr.

The Year of the Poet IV
July 2017

Featured Poets
Anca Mihaela Bruma
Ibaa Ismail
Zvonko Taneski

The Oak Moon

The Poetry Posse 2017

The Year of the Poet IV
August 2017

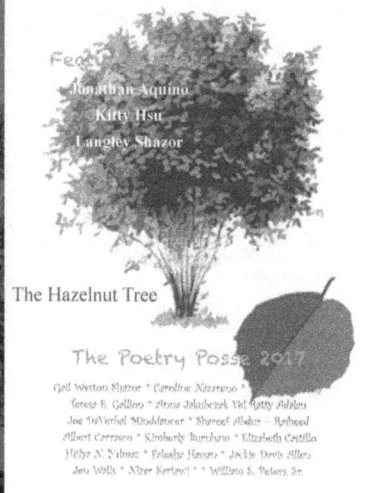

Featured Poets
Jonathan Aquino
Kitty Hsu
Langley Shazor

The Hazelnut Tree

The Poetry Posse 2017

Gail Weston Shazor * Caroline Nazareno *
Teresa E. Gallion * Anna Jakubczak Vel Ratty Adalan
Joe DaVerbal Minddancer * Shareef Abdur – Rasheed
Albert Carrasco * Kimberly Burnham * Elizabeth Castillo
Hülya N. Yılmaz * Pelasho Hassan * Jackie Davis Allen
Jan Wells * Nizar Sartawi * * William S. Peters, Sr.

Now Available

www.innerchildpress.com/the-year-of-the-poet

The Year of the Poet IV
September 2017

Featured Poets

Martina Reisz Newber

Ameer Nassir

Christine Fulco Neal

Robert Neal

The Elm Tree

The Poetry Posse 2017

Gail Weston Shazor * Caroline Nazareno * Bismay Mohanty
Teresa E. Gallion * Anna Jakubczak Vel Ratty Adalan
Joe DaVerbal Minddancer * Shareef Abdur – Rasheed
Albert Carrasco * Kimberly Burnham * Elizabeth Castillo
Hülya N. Yılmaz * Faleeha Hassan * Jackie Davis Allen
Jen Walls * Nizar Sartawi * * William S. Peters, Sr.

The Year of the Poet IV
October 2017

Featured Poets

Ahmed Abu Saleem

Nedal Al-Qaeim

Sadeddin Shahin

The Black Walnut Tree

The Poetry Posse 2017

Gail Weston Shazor * Caroline Nazareno * Bismay Mohanty
Teresa E. Gallion * Anna Jakubczak Vel Ratty Adalan
Joe DaVerbal Minddancer * Shareef Abdur – Rasheed
Albert Carrasco * Kimberly Burnham * Elizabeth Castillo
Hülya N. Yılmaz * Faleeha Hassan * Jackie Davis Allen
Jen Walls * Nizar Sartawi * * William S. Peters, Sr.

The Year of the Poet IV
November 2017

Featured Poets

Kay Peters

Alfreda D. Ghee

Gabriella Garofalo

Rosemary Cappello

The Tree of Life

The Poetry Posse 2017

Gail Weston Shazor * Caroline Nazareno * Bismay Mohanty
Teresa E. Gallion * Anna Jakubczak Vel Ratty Adalan
Joe DaVerbal Minddancer * Shareef Abdur – Rasheed
Albert Carrasco * Kimberly Burnham * Elizabeth Castillo
Hülya N. Yılmaz * Faleeha Hassan * Jackie Davis Allen
Jen Walls * Nizar Sartawi * William S. Peters, Sr.

The Year of the Poet IV
December 2017

Featured Poets

Justice Clarke

Mariel M. Pabroa

Kiley Brown

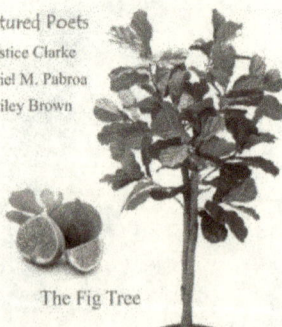

The Fig Tree

The Poetry Posse 2017

Gail Weston Shazor * Caroline Nazareno * Bismay Mohanty
Teresa E. Gallion * Anna Jakubczak Vel Ratty Adalan
Joe DaVerbal Minddancer * Shareef Abdur – Rasheed
Albert Carrasco * Kimberly Burnham * Elizabeth Castillo
Hülya N. Yılmaz * Faleeha Hassan * Jackie Davis Allen
Jen Walls * Nizar Sartawi * William S. Peters, Sr.

Now Available

www.innerchildpress.com/the-year-of-the-poet

The Year of the Poet V
January 2018

Featured Poets

Iyad Shamasnah
Yasmeen Hamzeh
Ali Abdolrezaei

Aksum

The Poetry Posse 2018

Gail Weston Shazor * Caroline Nazareno * Tezmin Ition Tsai
Hülya N. Yılmaz * Faleeha Hassan * Jackie Davis Allen
Teresa E. Gallion * Anna Jakubczak Vel Ratty Adalan
Alicja Maria Kubeska * Shareef Abdur – Rasheed
Kimberly Burnham * Elizabeth Castillo
Nizar Sartawi * William S. Peters, Sr.

The Year of the Poet V
February 2018

Sabean

Featured Poets

Muhammad Azram
Anna Szawrocka
Abhilipsa Kuanr
Aanika Aery

The Poetry Posse 2018

Gail Weston Shazor * Caroline Nazareno * Tezmin Ition Tsai
Hülya N. Yılmaz * Faleeha Hassan * Jackie Davis Allen
Teresa E. Gallion * Anna Jakubczak Vel Ratty Adalan
Alicja Maria Kubeska * Shareef Abdur – Rasheed
Kimberly Burnham * Elizabeth Castillo
Nizar Sartawi * William S. Peters, Sr.

The Year of the Poet V
March 2018

Featured Poets

Iram Fatima 'Ashi'
Cassandra Swan
Jaleel Khazaal
Shazia Zaman

Mexico   Cuba

Dominican
Republic

Belize   Jamaica   Haiti
Guatemala   Honduras   Puerto Rico
El Salvador   Nicaragua
Costa Rica   Panama

Caribbean
&
Middle America

Colombia

The Poetry Posse 2018

Gail Weston Shazor * Nizar Sartawi * Hülya N. Yılmaz
Jackie Davis Allen * Caroline 'Ceri' Nazareno
Alicja Maria Kubeska * Teresa E. Gallion
Faleeha Hassan * Shareef Abdur – Rasheed
Kimberly Burnham * Elizabeth Castillo
Tezmin Ition Tsai * William S. Peters, Sr.

The Year of the Poet V
April 2018

Featured Poets

The Nez Perce

The Poetry Posse 2018

Now Available

www.innerchildpress.com/the-year-of-the-poet

The Year of the Poet V
May 2018

Featured Poets

Zaldy Carreon de Leon Jr
Sylwia K. Malinowski
Liddita Ahmeti
Ofelia Preslav

The Sumerians

The Poetry Posse 2018

Gail Weston Shazor * Nizar Sartawi * Hülya N. Yılmaz
Jackie Davis Allen * Caroline 'Ceri' Nazareno
Alicja Maria Kubeńska * Teresa E. Gallion
Kimberly Burnham * Shareef Abdur – Rasheed
Faleeha Hassan * Elizabeth Castillo * Swapna Behera
Tezmin Ition Tsai * William S. Peters, Sr.

The Year of the Poet V
June 2018

Featured Poets

Bilall Maliqi * Daim Miftari * Gojko Božović * Sofija Živković

The Paleo Indians

The Poetry Posse 2018

Gail Weston Shazor * Nizar Sartawi * Hülya N. Yılmaz
Jackie Davis Allen * Caroline 'Ceri' Nazareno
Alicja Maria Kubeńska * Teresa E. Gallion
Kimberly Burnham * Shareef Abdur – Rasheed
Faleeha Hassan * Elizabeth Castillo * Swapna Behera
Tezmin Ition Tsai * William S. Peters, Sr.

The Year of the Poet V
July 2018

Featured Poets

Radwan Ittihage Daddy
Mohammad Bilal Hadi
Eliza Segiet
Tony Higgins

Oceania

The Poetry Posse 2018

Gail Weston Shazor * Nizar Sartawi * Hülya N. Yılmaz
Jackie Davis Allen * Caroline 'Ceri' Nazareno
Alicja Maria Kubeńska * Teresa E. Gallion
Kimberly Burnham * Shareef Abdur – Rasheed
Faleeha Hassan * Elizabeth Castillo * Swapna Behera
Tezmin Ition Tsai * William S. Peters, Sr.

The Year of the Poet V
August 2018

Featured Poets
Hussein Habasch * Mircea Dan Duta * Naida Mujkić * Swagat Das

The Lapita

The Poetry Posse 2018

Gail Weston Shazor * Nizar Sartawi * Hülya N. Yılmaz
Jackie Davis Allen * Caroline 'Ceri' Nazareno
Alicja Maria Kubeńska * Teresa E. Gallion
Kimberly Burnham * Shareef Abdur – Rasheed
Ashok K. Bhargava* Elizabeth Castillo * Swapna Behaera
Tezmin Ition Tsai * William S. Peters, Sr.

Now Available

www.innerchildpress.com/the-year-of-the-poet

The Year of the Poet V
September 2018

The Aztecs & Incas

Featured Poets
Kolade Olanrewaju Freedom
Elica Segut
Muslier Hussain Abdul Ghani
Lily Swarn

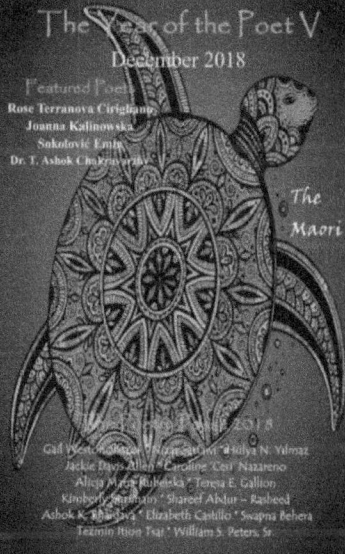

The Poetry Posse 2018

Gail Weston Shazor * Nizar Sartawi * Hülya N. Yılmaz
Jackie Davis Allen * Caroline 'Ceri' Nazareno
Alicja Maria Kuberska * Teresa E. Gallion
Kimberly Burnham * Shareef Abdur – Rasheed
Ashok K. Bhargava * Elizabeth Castillo * Swapna Behera
Tezmin Ition Tsai * William S. Peters, Sr.

The Year of the Poet V
October 2018

Featured Poets
Alicia Minjarez * Lonneice Weeks-Badley
Laxminadra Mishra * Abdelwahed Souayah

Bengali

The Poetry Posse 2018

Gail Weston Shazor * Nizar Sartawi * Hülya N. Yılmaz
Jackie Davis Allen * Caroline 'Ceri' Nazareno
Alicja Maria Kuberska * Teresa E. Gallion
Kimberly Burnham * Shareef Abdur – Rasheed
Ashok K. Bhargava * Elizabeth Castillo * Swapna Behera
Tezmin Ition Tsai * William S. Peters, Sr.

The Year of the Poet V
November 2018

Featured Poets
Michelle Joan Barulich * Monsif Beroual
Krystyna Konecka * Nassira Nezzar

The Poetry Posse 2018

The Year of the Poet V
December 2018

Featured Poets
Rose Terranova Cirigliano
Joanna Kalinowska
Sokolovic Emin
Dr. T. Ashok Chakravarthy

The Maori

Now Available

The Year of the Poet V I
January 2019

Indigenous North Americans

Featured Poets

Houda Elfchtali
Anthony Briscoe
Iram Fatima 'Ashi'
Dr. K. K. Mathew

Dream Catcher

The Poetry Posse 2019

Gail Weston Shazor * Joe Paire * Hülya N. Yılmaz
Jackie Davis Allen * Caroline 'Ceri' Nazareno
Alicja Maria Kubeska * Teresa E. Gallion
Kimberly Burnham * Shareef Abdur – Rasheed
Ashok K. Bhargava * Elizabeth Castillo * Swapna Behera
Tezmin Ition Tsai * William S. Peters, Sr.

The Year of the Poet VI
February 2019

Featured Poets

Marek Łukaszewicz * Bharati Nayak
Aida G. Roque * Jean-Jacques Fournier

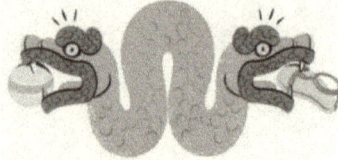

Meso–America

The Poetry Posse 2019

Gail Weston Shazor * Albert Carrasco * Hülya N. Yılmaz
Jackie Davis Allen * Caroline Nazareno * Eliza Segiet
Alicja Maria Kubeska * Teresa E. Gallion * Joe Paire
Kimberly Burnham * Shareef Abdur – Rasheed
Ashok K. Bhargava * Elizabeth Castillo * Swapna Behera
Tezmin Ition Tsai * William S. Peters, Sr.

The Year of the Poet VI
March 2019

Featured Poets

Enesa Mahmić * Sylwia K. Malinowska
Shurouk Hammoud * Anwer Ghani

The Caribbean

The Poetry Posse 2019

Gail Weston Shazor * Albert Carrasco * Hülya N. Yılmaz
Jackie Davis Allen * Caroline Nazareno * Eliza Segiet
Alicja Maria Kubeska * Teresa E. Gallion * Joe Paire
Kimberly Burnham * Shareef Abdur – Rasheed
Ashok K. Bhargava * Elizabeth Castillo * Swapna Behera
Tezmin Ition Tsai * William S. Peters, Sr.

The Year of the Poet VI
April 2019

Featured Poets

DL Davis * Michelle Joan Barulich
Lulëzim Haziri * Faleeha Hassan

Central & West Africa

The Poetry Posse 2019

Gail Weston Shazor * Albert Carrasco * Hülya N. Yılmaz
Jackie Davis Allen * Caroline Nazareno * Eliza Segiet
Alicja Maria Kubeska * Teresa E. Gallion * Joe Paire
Kimberly Burnham * Shareef Abdur – Rasheed
Ashok K. Bhargava * Elizabeth Castillo * Swapna Behera
Tezmin Ition Tsai * William S. Peters, Sr.

Now Available

www.innerchildpress.com/the-year-of-the-poet

The Year of the Poet VI
May 2019
Featured Poets
Emad Al-Haydary * Hussein Nasser Jabr
Wahab Sheriff * Abdul Razzaq Al Ameeri

Asia Southeast Asia and Maritime Asia

The Poetry Posse 2019
Gail Weston Shazor * Albert Carrasco * Hülya N. Yılmaz
Jackie Davis Allen * Caroline Nazareno * Eliza Segiet
Alicja Maria Kubeska * Teresa E. Gallion * Joe Paire
Kimberly Burnham * Shareef Abdur – Rasheed
Ashok K. Bhargava * Elizabeth Castillo * Swapna Behera
Tezmin Ition Tsai * William S. Peters, Sr.

The Year of the Poet VI
June 2019
Featured Poets
Kate Gaudi Powiekszone * Sahaj Sabharwal
Iwu Jeff * Mohamed Abdel Aziz Shmeis

Arctic
Circumpolar

The Poetry Posse 2019
Gail Weston Shazor * Albert Carrasco * Hülya N. Yılmaz
Jackie Davis Allen * Caroline Nazareno * Eliza Segiet
Alicja Maria Kubeska * Teresa E. Gallion * Joe Paire
Kimberly Burnham * Shareef Abdur – Rasheed
Ashok K. Bhargava * Elizabeth Castillo * Swapna Behera
Tezmin Ition Tsai * William S. Peters, Sr.

The Year of the Poet VI
Featured Poets
Saadeddin Shahin * Auriy Scott
Fabredin Stnche * Alok Kumar Ray

The Horn of Africa

Ethiopia   Djibouti

Somalia   Eritrea

The Poetry Posse 2019
Gail Weston Shazor * Albert Carrasco * Hülya N. Yılmaz
Jackie Davis Allen * Caroline Nazareno * Eliza Segiet
Alicja Maria Kubeska * Teresa E. Gallion * Joe Paire
Kimberly Burnham * Shareef Abdur – Rasheed
Ashok K. Bhargava * Elizabeth Castillo * Swapna Behera
Tezmin Ition Tsai * William S. Peters, Sr.

The Year of the Poet VI
August 2019
Featured Poets
Shola Balogun * Bharati Nayak
Monalisa Dash Dwibedy * Mbizo Chirasha

Coexist

Southwest Asia

The Poetry Posse 2019
Gail Weston Shazor * Albert Carrasco * Hülya N. Yılmaz
Jackie Davis Allen * Caroline Nazareno * Eliza Segiet
Alicja Maria Kubeska * Teresa E. Gallion * Joe Paire
Kimberly Burnham * Shareef Abdur – Rasheed
Ashok K. Bhargava * Elizabeth Castillo * Swapna Behera
Tezmin Ition Tsai * William S. Peters, Sr.

Now Available

www.innerchildpress.com/the-year-of-the-poet

The Year of the Poet VI
September 2019
Featured Poets
Elena Liliana Popescu * Gobinda Biswas
Iram Fatima 'Ashi' * Joseph S. Spence, Sr.

The Caucasus
The Poetry Posse 2019

Gail Weston Shazor * Albert Carrasco * Hülya N. Yılmaz
Jackie Davis Allen * Caroline Nazareno * Eliza Segiet
Alicja Maria Kuberska * Teresa E. Gallion * Joe Paire
Kimberly Burnham * Shareef Abdur – Rasheed
Ashok K. Bhargava * Elizabeth Castillo * Swapna Behera
Tezmin Ition Tsai * William S. Peters, Sr.

The Year of the Poet VI
October 2019
Featured Poets
Ngozi Olivia Osuoha * Denisa Kondić
Pankhori Sinha * Christena AV Williams

The Nile Valley
The Poetry Posse 2019

Gail Weston Shazor * Albert Carrasco * Hülya N. Yılmaz
Jackie Davis Allen * Caroline Nazareno * Eliza Segiet
Alicja Maria Kuberska * Teresa E. Gallion * Joe Paire
Kimberly Burnham * Shareef Abdur – Rasheed
Ashok K. Bhargava * Elizabeth Castillo * Swapna Behera
Tezmin Ition Tsai * William S. Peters, Sr.

The Year of the Poet VI
November 2019
Featured Poets
Rozalia Aleksandrova * Orbindu Ganga
Sronv Ranjan Mohanty * Sofia Skleida

Northern Asia
The Poetry Posse 2019

Gail Weston Shazor * Albert Carrasco * Hülya N. Yılmaz
Jackie Davis Allen * Caroline Nazareno * Eliza Segiet
Alicja Maria Kuberska * Teresa E. Gallion * Joe Paire
Kimberly Burnham * Shareef Abdur – Rasheed
Ashok K. Bhargava * Elizabeth Castillo * Swapna Behera
Tezmin Ition Tsai * William S. Peters, Sr.

The Year of the Poet VI
December 2019
Featured Poets
Robin Karim (Kazmov) * Bapân Pava
Bharad Nayak * Kapardeti Edtchra

Oceania

The Poetry Posse 2019

Gail Weston Shazor * Albert Carrasco * Hülya N. Yılmaz
Jackie Davis Allen * Caroline Nazareno * Eliza Segiet
Alicja Maria Kuberska * Teresa E. Gallion * Joe Paire
Kimberly Burnham * Shareef Abdur – Rasheed
Ashok K. Bhargava * Elizabeth Castillo * Swapna Behera
Tezmin Ition Tsai * William S. Peters, Sr.

Now Available

www.innerchildpress.com/the-year-of-the-poet

and there is much, much more !

visit . . .

www.innerchildpress.com/antho
logies-sales-special.php

Also check out our Authors and
all the wonderful Books
Available at :

www.innerchildpress.com/autho
rs-pages

INNER CHILD PRESS

WORLD HEALING WORLD PEACE
2018

A Poetry Anthology for Humanity

Now Available

www.worldhealingworldpeacepoetry.com

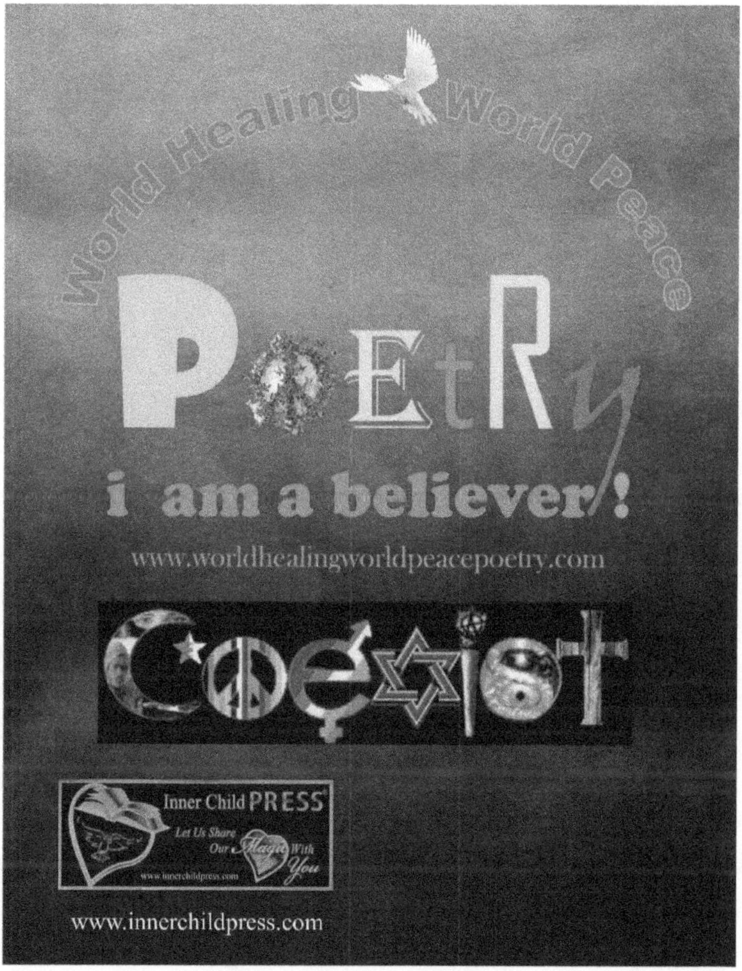

Now Available

www.worldhealingworldpeacepoetry.com

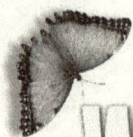

I support

World Healing World Peace

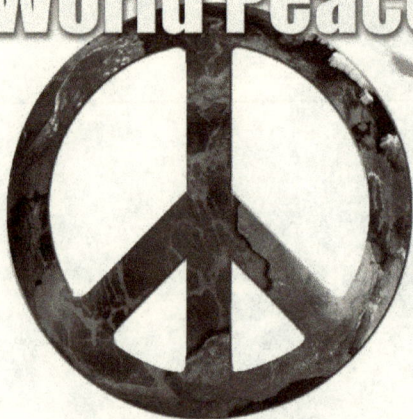

www.worldhealingworldpeacepoetry.com

World Healing World Peace
Po**E**t**R**y
i am a believer !

World Healing
World Peace
2018

Now Available

www.worldhealingworldpeacepoetry.com

Inner Child Press International

'building bridges of cultural understanding'

Meet our Cultural Ambassadors

Fabredas Shebu
Director of Cultural

Faleha Hassan
Iraq – USA

Elizabeth E. Castillo
Philippines

Antoinette Coleman
Chicago
Midwest USA

Ananda Nepali
Nepal – Hiot
acthout India

Kimberly Burnham
Pacific Northwest
USA

Alieja Kuberska
Poland
Eastern Europe

Swapna Behera
India
Southeast Asia

Kolade O. Freedom
Nigeria
West Africa

Mowxit Berouat
Morocco
Northern Afri.

Ashok K. Bhargava
Canada

Tzemin Ition Tsai
Republic of China
Greater China

Alicia M. Ramirez
Mexico
Central America

Christena AV Williams
Jamaica
Caribbean

Louise Hudon
Eastern Canada

Aziz Mountassir
Morocco
Western Africa

Shareef Abdur-Rasheed
Southeastern USA

Laure Charazac
France
Western Europe

Mohammad Ikbal Harb
Lebanon
Middle East

Mohamed Abdel
Aziz Shmeis
Egypt
Middle East

Hilary Mainga
Kenya
Eastern Africa

Josephus R. Johnson
Liberia

www.innerchildpress.com

197

This Anthological Publication
is underwritten solely by

Inner Child Press

Inner Child Press is a Publishing Company Founded and Operated by Writers. Our personal publishing experiences provides us an intimate understanding of the sometimes daunting challenges Writers, New and Seasoned may face in the Business of Publishing and Marketing their Creative "Written Work".

For more Information

Inner Child Press

www.innerchildpress.com

Inner Child Press International
'building bridges of cultural understanding'
202 Wiltree Court, State College, Pennsylvania 16801

www.innerchildpress.com

~ *fini* ~